APPROACHING
BIBLICAL ARCHAEOLOGY

APPROACHING BIBLICAL ARCHAEOLOGY

ANTHONY J. FRENDO

t&tclark

LONDON · NEW YORK · OXFORD · NEW DELHI · SYDNEY

T&T CLARK
Bloomsbury Publishing Plc
50 Bedford Square, London, WC1B 3DP, UK
1385 Broadway, New York, NY 10018, USA
29 Earlsfort Terrace, Dublin 2, Ireland

BLOOMSBURY, T&T CLARK and the T&T Clark logo
are trademarks of Bloomsbury Publishing Plc

First published in Great Britain 2022
Reprinted 2022

A catalogue record for this book is available from the British Library.

Library of Congress Cataloging-in-Publication Data
Names: Frendo, Anthony J., author.
Title: Approaching biblical archaeology / Anthony J. Frendo.
Description: London ; New York : T&T Clark, 2021. | Includes bibliographical references and index.
| Summary: "A concise introduction to biblical archaeology, covering the bible in its ancient context
and broader cultural milieu and introducing the discipline of archaeology to biblicists"--
Provided by publisher.
Identifiers: LCCN 2021004236 (print) | LCCN 2021004237 (ebook) |
ISBN 9780567677532 (paperback) | ISBN 9780567676993 (hardback) |
ISBN 9780567677006 (pdf) | ISBN 9780567701558 (epub)
Subjects: LCSH: Bible--Antiquities. | Archaeology. | Archaeology and history.
Classification: LCC BS621 .F733 2021 (print) | LCC BS621 (ebook) | DDC 220.9/3--dc23
LC record available at https://lccn.loc.gov/2021004236
LC ebook record available at https://lccn.loc.gov/2021004237

ISBN: HB: 978-0-5676-7699-3
         PB   978-0-5676-7753-2
         ePDF: 978-0-5676-7700-6
         ePUB: 978-0-5677-0155-8

Typeset by Trans.form.ed SAS
Printed and bound in Great Britain

To find out more about our authors and books visit www.bloomsbury.com and sign up
for our newsletters.

To my dearest Lillian, a virtuous woman,

a prime example of the אשת חיל in Prov. 31.10a

CONTENTS

ACKNOWLEDGEMENTS

As happens with so many publications, this monograph took much longer to come into existence than I originally anticipated. Although I have been lecturing for the past thirty-one years on many of the topics dealt with in this book, I undertook the bulk of the research directly pertinent to it during my sabbatical, from October 2018 to September 2019. In this regard, I would like to thank the University of Malta for granting me sabbatical leave, as well as Dr Abigail R. Zammit and Dr Omar N'Shea, both of whom very kindly took on my teaching duties for the academic year 2018–19, with the former taking the brunt.

Since in reality this monograph is also the fruit of three decades of teaching, a special thanks must go to my students (some of whom are now friends and colleagues at this University), who over the years have shown great interest and enthusiasm, and who above all posed many intelligent questions. I would also like to thank the Academic Work Resources Fund Committee at the University of Malta, without whose financial aid I would not have been able to go annually to Oxford to carry out research in those most well-equipped libraries, especially the Bodleian, the Sackler, and the Oriental Institute library, which is where I carried out most of my work. A special thanks goes to Mrs Diane Bergman, former librarian at the Sackler library, who often came to my rescue when I needed to pin down certain items that required specialist help.

I should certainly not forget to mention my friends at Oxford University whom I always enjoyed talking to and from whom I have learnt so much. Special thanks go to professors *emeriti* H.G.M. Williamson (Christ Church), John Day (Lady Margaret Hall), John Barton (Oriel College), and Dr Stephanie Dalley (Honorary Senior Research Fellow, Somerville College), all of the University of Oxford, and to Emeritus Professor Kevin J. Cathcart of University College, Dublin, but who was often at Oxford teaching and doing research work there. Hearty thanks go to Dr Patrik Flammer, a post-doctoral research assistant in the Department of Zoology at the University of Oxford, who helped me a great deal to understand what archaeoparasitology is all about. It is essentially thanks to him that I could draw up with a reasonable amount of confidence my comments in Chapter 5 about the contribution that archaeoparasitology is making to our knowledge about the last days of Judah in 586 BCE. When in Oxford I generally stayed at Campion Hall, and I would also like to thank the Masters and my friends there for always making my stay at the Hall comfortable and pleasant.

I thank Mr Dominic Mattos, Editorial Director and Publisher at Bloomsbury T&T Clark, for having taken the time to attend to the manuscript of this monograph, for his editorial advice, and for accepting the manuscript for publication. Thanks also to Ms Sarah Blake, Assistant Editor at Bloomsbury T&T Clark, and to Ms Jessica Anderson, the Production Editor of this monograph, and to their copyediting team, especially to Dr Duncan Burns, who also compiled the indices.

I would also like to thank the two anonymous reviewers whose observations, critical remarks, and suggestions I appreciate. Indeed, those comments that were more critical were the ones which helped me to enhance my own text. I obviously take full responsibility for any shortcomings in this work.

Last but not least I thank my beloved wife, Lillian, who always stood by me, patiently listening to what I had to say and supporting me along the way. To her I dedicate this work.

University of Malta, Tal-Qroqq, Msida, Malta

September 2020

PREFACE

It is a well-known fact that many books can be tagged with the words "Biblical Archaeology". Unfortunately, however, some of them are out "to prove the Bible true" by relating the results of biblical research with those of the relevant archaeological discoveries in the wrong way, namely without really following the rules of interpretation of the two respective fields, above all by not reading the Bible critically. However, we should not lose sight of the fact that there are also a substantial number of very good publications on "Biblical Archaeology". Such, for example, is the case with *The Bible & Archaeology* (only recently published in English), whose author, Matthieu Richelle,[1] succeeds in giving a very good overview of the field of "Biblical Archaeology" in a clear, concise, and precise manner, without endorsing any extreme position: neither that of fundamentalism nor that of relativism.

So why write another monograph on the Bible and Archaeology? Despite the fact that books like the one just mentioned are very good and that they do demonstrate cogent thinking when it comes to amalgamating the results of archaeological research with those of biblical criticism, still there seems to be a gap in the sense that biblical scholars are not really shown *how* they themselves can make their own judgement in deciding whether the results that archaeologists hand over to them are reliable. For them to do this they need to be aware of the thought processes of archaeologists and how the latter reach their conclusions.

Hence, in this monograph I do not aim to give a history of Biblical Archaeology, and much less do I purport to give an exhaustive list of interesting archaeological discoveries that have a bearing on the Bible. The primary aim of this study is to introduce biblical students and scholars alike to how

---

[1] Richelle 2018.

the minds of professional archaeologists work, namely by explaining what the latter seek, how they go about doing their work, and how they interpret their data. But this does not mean that this book is an introduction to the discipline of archaeology describing the various latest techniques that archaeologists employ—on that subject there are multiple excellent publications, a few of which I mention in Chapter 2. Neither is this monograph an introduction to the study of the Bible; the publications on this topic are legion, and biblical students and scholars who constitute the main target audience of this book are acquainted with them.

What I am aiming at in this book is to single out a number of basic, elementary aspects of archaeology, such as stratigraphic excavation, good scientific dating techniques, report writing that does not confuse the data with their interpretation, and the use of ceramic chronology (despite its possible pitfalls). Together, these elements represent the *sine qua non* for archaeologists. These aspects are discussed in order to give those engaged in the field of biblical studies a better understanding of how archaeologists reach their conclusions. The examples provided in Chapters 2 to 6 each illustrate one theme that helps to show how biblical research and archaeology can work with each other in a valid and worthwhile manner. Although the concrete examples in Chapters 2 to 6 provide illustrations of Biblical Archaeology, above all they focus on a methodological discussion of the interpretative processes involved in bringing the archaeological and biblical data together in meaningful dialogue.

Although some of the examples that I mention or analyze happen to match certain information found in the Bible, in no way does this mean that my agenda is to prove the Bible right. Chapter 6 testifies to this in a very clear way. Some readers could get the wrong impression, if they concentrate only on the examples that I present in Chapter 1. I underscore the fact that the examples in that chapter are simply *introductory summaries* of examples of Biblical

Archaeology. These are offered as "tasters" of the methodological issues that are involved in the other examples that I study in detail in Chapters 2 to 6.

In this book I use the word "Bible" mainly with reference to the Hebrew Bible, although in some instances I do give a few examples from the Christian New Testament.

The book will show those engaged in biblical scholarship how they can properly integrate biblical research with archaeological discoveries in a way that allows the Bible and archaeology to be viewed and kept as distinct disciplines, the respective results of which, however, should, where relevant, be integrated without resulting in a "mishmash". There will also be a discussion of how the archaeology of the ancient Near East (particularly that of the southern Levant) has an essential bearing on how scholars can better appreciate the text of the Bible, including its religious message.

In order to reach the aforementioned aims, I select some of the most basic nuts and bolts of archaeology and, above all, of archaeological reasoning, illustrating each of them with an example. I focus on a number of basic themes that characterize archaeology and deal with them in such a way that biblical scholars can make their own judgement as to whether the information that archaeologists relay to them is reliable or not. That is why, for example, after a brief general description of what the discipline of archaeology aims to accomplish and of the distinction between archaeological data and their interpretation (Chapter 2), I deal with such matters as artefacts (Chapter 3), stratigraphy and chronology (Chapter 4), and archaeological reasoning (Chapter 5). Although generally it is archaeology that casts light on the biblical text, allowing us to better appreciate the latter, in Chapter 6 I deal with the fact that in practice we can actually have a two-way flow of "traffic": not only can archaeology make a contribution to biblical interpretation, but text-based biblical exegesis can help us in understanding certain data retrieved in archaeological excavations. One example that I discuss at length in Chapter 6 is how the biblical text can help us to understand better the phrase "Yahweh and his Asherah", which surfaced in the excavations at Kuntillet 'Ajrud.

As already mentioned above, the target audience of this monograph is primarily students and scholars of the Bible. While archaeologists will surely learn nothing new from this book about their techniques, it is my hope that it will help them to be more *critically* conscious of what is really involved when scholars try to relate non-written with written evidence. Moreover, in no way do I mean to exclude those amongst the wider public who are interested in either of the fields of the Bible or that of archaeology, especially inasmuch as these two disciplines can throw light on each other. Indeed, for this reason I have done my my utmost to keep the style of writing as clear and simple as possible, avoiding jargon. Inevitably there were instances when I had to use a technical term (which is not the same thing as jargon); however, in these cases I always made sure to define and/or clarify such terms—usually in a footnote. Since the wider public is included in the target audience of this monograph, I listed all the bibliographical works using the succinct "author–date" system,[2] placing in footnotes the particular references to the respective publications, the full details of which can be found in the Bibliography. In this way, readers can easily ignore the notes and references if they so chose. They will notice that the following chapters vary in length—this is true especially with respect to Chapter 4, which is significantly longer than all the other chapters. However, this should not constitute a problem because, just as "no absolute rules regulate a paragraph's length, since its size is a function of the arrangement and flow of the text it contains",[3] the same holds true for the length of chapters.

The variegated target audience of this book justifies my explaining certain terms and issues in archaeology that archaeologists know so well and for whom they constitute elementary concepts. The same logic supports my

[2]For an explanation of the "author–date" system see Ritter 2002: 566–72.
[3]Ritter 2002: 18.

clarifying a number of terms and themes pertinent to biblical studies that hardly need explaining to students and scholars engaged in that field. In view of this, general readers are strongly encouraged to read the whole monograph, since only then will it become clear what I mean by the above-mentioned phrase "*critically* conscious". Again, the goal of this book is to help formulate a way of working that avoids biblical and archaelogical data being brought together as a "mishmash" of results.

Readers who do not know Classical Hebrew should not be put off reading this book. While I make numerous references to Hebrew terms (mainly in Chapter 6), I have avoided using the Hebrew script, opting instead for the use of transliteration. Transliteration, it is hoped, will allow the general reader to hold on to the thread of reasoning used by biblical specialists. The whole point of this book is to help primarily those interested in relating the Bible to archaeology to understand how archaeologists and biblical specialists think, and how they reach their conclusions.

It is my hope that biblical scholars and students, as well as readers from the general public, will in turn be able to make their own judgements as to whether or not the results that archaeologists pass on to them are reliable. They will then be in a much better position to integrate the results of biblical research with those of the relevant archaeological investigations. That is why I titled this monograph *Approaching Biblical Archaeology*.

I hope that this labour of love, which took much longer to finish than I had first anticipated, will help others to be not only insightful but also *critically* so in view of the fact that "all men have a reason, but not all men can give a reason".[4] My wish is that, after reading this monograph, readers will become accustomed to asking themselves explicitly the following crucial question: What did the excavators actually find? Sometimes it might be very difficult to answer this question, if not well-nigh impossible. However, the

---

[4]Newman 1871: xi.

examples discussed in Chapter 2 show that it is possible to pose and answer the question, therefore confirming that the question is a legitimate one. Only after answering such a question shall we be able to relate in a methodologically proper manner our interpretation of the biblical data with that of the relevant archaeological ones.

1

Introduction

As already mentioned in the Preface, there are many publications dealing with the topic of "The Bible and Archaeology". However, within this popular genre there are hardly any works that aim to introduce students of the Bible to the discipline of archaeology, with the primary aim of showing them *how* to integrate the results of archaeology with those of biblical scholarship. As all students and scholars of the Bible worth their salt know, relating the results of biblical scholarship with those of archaeology is a *sine qua non* and not a luxury. However, the problem is to ensure that this is done in a proper way. This book aims precisely at helping those engaged with the biblical text to ask the right sort of questions when reading about the results that archaeologists of the ancient Near East (especially of the southern Levant) pass on to them.

Students of the Bible need to know not only the basics of their scholarly field, but also those of archaeology. Yet, engaging with the archaeological data should not be attempted in an unrestrained fashion—it is for this reason that the present work is titled *Approaching Biblical Archaeology*. Students of the Bible are introduced to how the minds of archaeologists work, giving them insight into what mental processes are involved in the interpretation of retrieved data, so that one can then compare and contrast these activities with those of biblical scholars. Biblical Archaeology is legitimate as long as it tackles the Bible according to the rules of biblical scholarship, and archaeology according to the methods of archaeological research, and only thereafter compares and contrasts any interpretation of the biblical data with that of the archaeological data.[1] In general, archaeology throws a great deal of light on the cultural background and customs that we find in the pages of the Bible. However, there are times when archaeology can also make a contribution to the central message of the Bible when it happens to illuminate the background context of certain texts, the core statements of which are of a religious nature.

Chapter 2 presents a very basic overview of archaeology, one that underscores the distinction between the data that archaeologists retrieve and their interpretation of those data. It aims to show how archaeologists reach their conclusions and that it is only via correct interpretation of the data that they are able to say what was really found on a site. This process, however, is cumulative. It is seldom the case that we reach a correct conclusion at the first attempt, simply by attending to the details of the data. It is a process that takes time and which involves a good deal of reflection as we pass through various, different, and often conflicting interpretations. However, neither does this mean that all interpretations are correct or equally probable. It happens that the data retrieved in an excavation do not always warrant the conclusions that certain archaeologists reach and which they promote in the popular media. Biblical scholars would do well to always ask the question: What did the excavators actually find?

In the following chapter it will be shown that writing itself is a technology and that consequently all written products are also to be viewed as artefacts since they are not the result of natural processes but of man-made ones. This chapter will thus take into consideration the fact that all artefacts, both those we use in daily life as well as those found in archaeological investigations, can be broadly divided into written and unwritten; indeed, the Bible itself is an

---

[1]De Vaux 1970: 70, 78.

artefact. We should aim at integrating the results of the analyses of all types of artefacts, whether they are unearthed in archaeological excavations or not and whether they happen to be inscribed or not. We need to make use of *all* available data, since this will help us to better understand all types of artefacts from antiquity. An integrated approach is the only way for us to obtain a more secure gateway into the past.

In Chapter 4, I shall discuss two essential hallmarks of archaeological research, namely stratigraphic excavation and ceramic studies. These will be shown to be particularly important for their bearing on chronological problems. The peeling off of the layers on a site in the reverse order to that in which they were laid down is precisely what ensures the validity of a relative chronology, which when pegged to data yielding chronometric dates is extremely useful for interpreting the past. Students of the Bible need to be aware of the distinction between reliable and unreliable findspots since this allows them to appreciate critically whether certain archaeological finds can be *reliably linked* with the pertinent information found in the Bible. As a case study for this chapter, I shall take the current debate on the chronology of the transition from the Early Iron Age to Iron Age II in ancient Israel. The results of this chronological debate will determine whether we can view the kingdom of Israel in Solomon's time as something to be reckoned with or simply as a virtually insignificant entity.

The aforementioned case study also shows how important it is to relate in a proper manner the results of biblical research with those of archaeology. Hence in Chapter 5 I shall argue that in the first instance the biblical data and the archaeological data have to be studied separately according to their respective methods of research. It is only thereafter that our biblical interpretation can be compared and contrasted with our archaeological one relative to the same problem under investigation. When the two interpretations are brought together, they help to offer us a more complete gateway to the past, and hence to our understanding of the Bible itself. Notwithstanding this, however, at times it is inevitable for students of the Bible to use the results of archaeology before they have independently given the biblical "answer" to a question and vice versa. This can clearly lead to a circular argument, that is, reading the Bible in the light of archaeology and then proceeding to read the latter in the light of the Bible. This is a classic example of the hermeneutic circle that can only be broken if time and time again we seek to verify our claims in the light of a fresh analysis of the data. I shall illustrate these points by showing how biblical scholars have been influenced by archaeologists in their understanding of the Hebrew term *bāmāh* (commonly rendered as "high place") and how, in turn, archaeologists were influenced by biblical scholars when pinning down "high places" in their excavations. Only a re-reading of the data can show us the way out of this impasse. However, I shall also look at one clear example of how archaeological and biblical evidence can be brought to bear on each other without the use of any circular arguments. I am referring to the analysis of the faecal remains from a sixth-century BCE toilet in Jerusalem that shows clearly how dire the situation of the inhabitants of Jerusalem must have been during the siege of the Babylonians—just as described in Lamentations.

In the sixth chapter I shall argue that the points discussed in the previous chapters help students of the Bible to understand it better. Yet I shall also proceed to show that, when it comes to Biblical Archaeology, in practice we are dealing with a two-way flow of traffic, namely with archaeology throwing light on the Bible but also with cases when the latter helps us to solve conundrums arising from certain data retrieved in archaeological excavations. I shall first adduce other instances of how archaeology can throw light on the Bible, specifically on how it can contribute to our better grasping the semantics of the biblical text in view of the fact that meaning involves matters other than those that are purely language bound. Then I shall discuss an example of how the Bible (in this case Deut. 33:2) can help us to untangle certain difficulties that the archaeological data pose. I specifically tackle at length the problems raised by the phrase "Yahweh and *šrth*" present in some of the inscriptions from Kuntillet ʿAjrud. It will be shown that in reality it is highly probable that *šrth* is in fact referring to the goddess Asherah herself, and that the pronominal suffix with a divine name should cause no grammatical problem, for various reasons including the highly interesting results of a very recent work in comparative Semitic studies.[2]

Finally, in the concluding chapter I shall highlight three main conclusions reached in this book: (1) that knowledge of the archaeology of the Levant (indeed possibly of the ancient Near East in general) and knowing how to integrate it properly with biblical studies is a must for the student of the Bible; (2) that archaeology can help the student of the Bible not only to understand the background of the Bible better but to get a better grasp of the biblical text itself; and (3) that the priority for students of the Bible vis-à-vis archaeology is to grasp how they can (in an independent and critical manner) decide whether or not the claims made in archaeological reports and in books on the Bible and Archaeology are trustworthy.

In order to discuss properly all the topics mentioned above, I would like to first highlight in a summary fashion some examples of Biblical Archaeology that go to show the crucial things that biblical scholars would do well to be on the lookout for when it comes to incorporating the results of archaeological research in their interpretation of the biblical text. This will help the readers of this monograph to see for themselves what Biblical Archaeology really involves and at the same time to appreciate that this field is not a luxury for biblical scholars but an essential part of their quest to interpret the biblical texts.

First of all, we should remind ourselves that archaeologists are not simply technicians; indeed, first and foremost they should know how to interpret their finds. As J.A. Wilson wrote: "Mere measurement is not enough; he [the

---

[2]Stein 2019.

archaeologist] must bring to his excavation a keen sense of values".[3] In this sense it is preferable to have "a properly *evaluated* dig than one in which every object is precisely weighed and measured but stands isolated in mere bulk".[4] Archaeologists should—just like all scholars worthy of the name—first and foremost be dedicated to understanding their data and to verifying their insights rather than to perceiving themselves as belonging to some debating society. They do not seek to defend any bias or predetermined thesis that they might have, but to *earnestly look for* meaning in the data that they unearth; indeed, "one ascertained fact outweighs a thousand unsupported doubts of the hypercritic".[5] A.T. Olmstead had reminded us that the Greek words *historeo* and *skeptomai*, which provide the origins of the English words "historian" and "sceptic" respectively, have in essence one and the same basic meaning, namely "to inquire/examine".[6] I am pointing this out because of the current intellectual climate that is at times unduly hypercritical and sceptical (in the sense of the contemporary meaning of this word) when it comes to biblical texts. It is a commonplace that at times too much is asked of the biblical text; as such, there is a demand for empirical proof that, many think, archaeology should provide. In the event that archaeology is not in a position to provide such proof, there follows a suspicion that we should doubt the text. Such a stance is not warranted, since no matter how limited our textual documentation may be, on condition that we sift all the data carefully, minutely, and critically, "the only limits it [the textual documentation] imposes on us are to set reasonable limits to our own skepticism".[7]

All this implies that we have to examine *all* the available data very carefully, and in the field of Biblical Archaeology this requires an examination of the textual *and* archaeological evidence. All types of relevant data have to be

---

[3] Wilson 1942: 6.
[4] Wilson 1942: 7 (my italics).
[5] Olmstead 1943: 5.
[6] Olmstead 1943: 6.
[7] Hallo 1990: 199.

interpreted; indeed, there is a distinction between data and knowledge, and in this monograph this will be borne out all along. Thus, for example, there is no direct correspondence between an ash layer and a destructive conflagration, since a significant accumulation of ash could very well be the result of sustained domestic combustion (for cooking and heating purposes). The decision we make in this regard is the result of interpretation, since to reach a conclusion as to whether we are dealing with destruction or domestic burning we need to compare the ash layer with other data and the overall context.[8] Indeed, "the evidence does not speak objectively for itself. It must be classified and compared with other evidence before we can use it."[9]

So, biblical archaeologists have to examine very carefully both the biblical and the archaeological evidence. Unfortunately this was not always the case and that is why Biblical Archaeology "has all too often been assessed rather more than is just [*sic*] from its popular idiocies and blatant shortcomings"; yet the truth is that "there has been, as there will always continue to be, good, bad and indifferent research and scholarship in biblical archaeology, as in any academic discipline; but it will remain unusually vulnerable to prejudice".[10] It is clear that Biblical Archaeology is an interdisciplinary subject and consequently it demands that its practitioners exercise great caution and academic rigour. Biblical archaeology can be compared to a "'shopping cart' that collects data from the various branches of Near Eastern Archaeology and utilizes them in studying the Bible in its world".[11]

The foregoing point implies that biblical archaeologists have to deal in an especial manner with the integration of textual and unwritten evidence, thereby also attempting to gain a more comprehensive historical knowledge of the past. In doing this, they make use of typology by detecting "those traits

---

[8]Brandfon 1987: 33, 34.
[9]Brandfon 1987: 33.
[10]Moorey 1991: xvi.
[11]Mazar 2007a: 33.

which are *common* to numerous concrete phenomena", which means that they cannot be satisfied with simply describing their data.[12] On the contrary, they have to do their utmost to reveal the "concrete cultural phenomena in their interdependence, their causal conditions and their *significance*".[13] All this means that biblical archaeologists have to be at the cutting edge of interdisciplinary research.

In recent years the discipline of Biblical Archaeology has been embroiled in the discussion between the so-called maximalists and minimalists. These labels are used (sometimes without due caution) to describe respectively those who largely believe that the Hebrew Bible was composed before the Babylonian Exile and that it contains historically reliable information (the "maximalists"), and those who, on the contrary, claim that the Hebrew Bible is a post-exilic creation devoid of hardly any reliable historical information (the "minimalists"). I have already observed elsewhere that it is preferable to avoid name-calling and to refrain from even using these terms[14] since what we really need to distinguish is between "good and bad historians, and both kinds are to be found on either side of the scholarly debate".[15] In fact, the aforementioned labels can mislead us into forgetting that in Biblical Archaeology too we must examine case by case and that we should refrain from making generalizations. We need to step back from those theoretical discussions that have long forgotten the solid launching pad of the pertinent data and take a fresh, hard look at the latter. If we do this, we can appreciate much better what we are really dealing with and that there are clear cases that vouch for historically reliable traditions that emerged in the pre-exilic period.[16] Thus, for example,

---

[12]Weber 1949: 92 (italics original).

[13]Weber 1949: 92 (italics original).

[14]Frendo 2011: 105.

[15]Na'aman 2006: 10.

[16]For a still-valid discussion regarding the existence or otherwise of Israel before 586 BCE, see the essays in Day 2004. For a critical overview on the specific problem of the emergence of Israel in the pre-Exilic period, see my essay there (Frendo 2004). These references can help readers to put in their proper context the examples that I discuss in the remainder of this chapter.

it is hardly a coincidence that the tribal boundaries and royal districts that we encounter in the Hebrew Bible match very closely the "settlement patterns and historical realities in the eighth and seventh centuries B.C.E.".[17] This conclusion does not simply tell us when the texts dealing with the tribal boundaries and royal districts originated; it also provides another instance that goes to show that there was a pre-exilic Israel.

To succeed in doing Biblical Archaeology in a sound manner we would do well to double our efforts in paying a great deal of attention to detail in all our areas of research. Indeed, "unless serious attention is given to details, all theories about the whole can only be castles in the air".[18] Sound familiarity with the biblical data, for example, can even help us to "solve" certain questions that are still considered to be moot by archaeologists. Thus, the archaeology of the Early Iron Age (roughly corresponding to the biblical period of the Judges) indicates the nature of Israelite society during this period, allowing us to predict that a more hierarchical type of society (such as the Monarchy) would emerge. However, for this to occur there had to be "a specific catalyst", which in this case turned out to be Saul. In this regard, the narrative in 1 Samuel 11 is of great interest since we see here that Saul rose to power in response to a threat from the Ammonites and that this in turn led the Philistines to "take steps to counter the rise of the new threat (*not* vice versa, as has been often and influentially suggested in the past)".[19] This scenario helps us to appreciate better the fact that towards the beginning of the first millennium BCE there arose a kingdom in Israel that was already back then a force to be reckoned with, one that would be all the more powerful by Solomon's time. This factor

---

[17]Finkelstein 2007: 13.

[18]Hurvitz 1997: 301. Here Hurvitz tells us that this saying is attributed to W. von Humboldt without giving any further precise information regarding the original source, which to date I was not able to trace. I also asked a doctoral student at the Humboldt University of Berlin to check this issue with an expert on W. von Humboldt there; unfortunately, the reply was that the latter scholar was not aware of any link between the saying in question and Humboldt.

[19]Williamson 2015: 6.

should be included in the archaeological debate surrounding the existence or otherwise of a sizeable kingdom in Solomon's time, something that I shall tackle in Chapter 4.

An authentic (albeit bought on the antiques market) Egyptian text on a plinth relief (Relief ÄM 21687) that had been procured by L. Borchardt for the Egyptian Museum in Berlin has inscribed on it the name "Israel". It is highly interesting to note that the word "Israel" is here written in a shorter variant than the larger form extant on the famous stela of Merneptah (1207 BCE),[20] which it predates. The Egyptian text turns out to be of the utmost importance for the very earliest history of the emergence of ancient Israel in Canaan.[21] In fact, this inscribed plinth shows us that we can now take the date of c. 1250 BCE as the start of the Early Iron Age whilst observing an overlap of about one hundred years between it and the end of the Late Bronze Age, namely 1160/1150 BCE.[22] This overlap thus covers the emergence of the highland villages in central Canaan and the demise of the city-state culture of the southern Levant. Indeed, "die neue Inschrift kann als Anlass genommen werden, über die absolute Chronologie zur Entstehung der Eisenzeit I und die Überlappung von spätbronzezeithlichen und eisenzeitlichen Kultur bzw.

[20]Not all scholars agree that the word "Israel" on the Merneptah Stela denotes a group of people; some have strong reason to believe that this word here stands for a geographical area. Be that as it may, this word is important for the very early history of Israel, since the people linked to an area labelled "Israel" would be Israelites. See Spiegelberg 1908; Engel 1979: 386; and Frendo 2004: 53, where I had concluded that "the general opinion that in Merneptah's stele Israel stands for an unsettled people rather than for a land should—to say the least—be viewed simply as one possible hypothesis and not even the more probable one".

[21]Veen and Zwickel 2014: 425–7. For a more recent study on the Berlin Relief ÄM 21687, see Zwickel and Veen 2017. P. van der Veen informed me in an email dated 29th May 2017 that "there are no determinatives on the Berlin relief, neither for towns nor for people. The second name ring (centre) reads Kanaanu, which probably refers to Canaanites and hence would be comparable with Israel/Israelites. Both lack determinatives for people but so does Ashkelon which lacks the town determinative." Zwickel and Veen (2017: 129 and references there) remind us that Manfred Görg had originally proposed to read on the Berliln Relief ÄM 21687 "a fragmentary preserved topographical or regional name as Israel" and they endorse this reading as a "convincing proposal" since "likely it will never be possible to completely ascertain this reading" (ibid.: 130–1).

[22]Veen and Zwickel 2014: 429. Note, however, that in their more recent study (Zwickel and Veen 2017: 137) they place the overlap in question between 1350 BCE and 1140 BCE.

von Niedergang der Statdtkultur und dem Enstehen neuer Siedlungen im Bergland neu nachzudenken".[23] The great attention to detail that P.G. van der Veen and W. Zwickel gave to the Egyptian inscribed relief ÄM 21687 helps in placing the emergence of Israel in the hill country of the southern Levant in a better context. Indeed, it goes to show that there is a seemingly direct correlation and an overlap between the demise of the Late Bronze Age city culture of southern Canaan and the sprouting of many village settlements in the hilly areas of this region in the Early Iron Age.

The aforementioned phenomenon of the emergence of ancient Israel in the hill country of the southern Levant is rather difficult to pin down in the archaeological record, and in this context once again it is attention to detail and accurate scholarship that can lead us on the right path. M.D. Coogan reminds us that the identity card of the early Israelites was their faith in Yahweh, something that is virtually impossible to infer from the artefacts that archaeologists generally retrieve in the Early Iron Age strata of the southern Levant. Hence, we see, for example, that the type of house that was very popular in the Levant during the Iron Age and that is generally known as the four-room house cannot lead us to simply conclude that we are dealing with the ancient Israelites every time we unearth such a type of house. As Coogan aptly writes: "But if we were to excavate the remains of contemporary houses in Jebus, Bethlehem, and Gibea, would we be able to ascertain from the surviving ruins which house was Israelite and which was 'foreign' (i.e., non-Israelite)? Without the presence of written remains identifying the owner of a house as Yahwistic I think not."[24]

The problem besetting the historicity or otherwise of pre-exilic Israel that was briefly mentioned above is well known, and it is found in many areas of research into the Hebrew Bible. In fact, the sheer amount of discussion given to this topic should remind us to be very wary before concluding that

[23]Veen and Zwickel 2014: 429.
[24]Coogan 1987: 6.

we cannot really speak of Israel in pre-exilic times. Thus, for example, Israel Finkelstein correctly notes that the biblical stories regarding David and his band roaming around southern Judah fit rather neatly with what we know of the bands of 'Apiru.[25] Indeed, this scenario does not fit the late monarchic period and much less so the post-exilic one when the 'Apiru were no longer in existence and when the area in question was densely populated.[26] This simply means that such stories about David are highly likely to have originated some time before the late monarchic period at the latest. The same conclusion holds good for the importance of Shiloh, a city which appears in the first book of Samuel. The archaeology of this site teaches us that it reached the pinnacle of its importance in the late eleventh century BCE, and that all through Iron Age II it witnessed "only meager activity".[27] Indeed, Shiloh was destroyed in the second half of the eleventh century BCE and was only resettled in the Byzantine period.[28] Shiloh's destruction in the Iron Age was "dramatic", and this event greatly affected the "Israelite common memory" to such an extent that in the Hebrew Bible "Shiloh" became a cipher for destruction (Jer. 7:12, 14; 26:6, 9).[29] Moreover, the archaeological evidence also strongly points in the direction that Shiloh was an Israelite settlement in the early Iron Age since its material culture is identical to other central hill country settlements "which were also settled by Israelites".[30]

The archaeology of Gath points in an analogous direction. In this case, the height of this site's activity is evidenced in the ninth century BCE. We also know that Gath was engulfed by flames in the latter part of this century,

---

[25]The 'Apiru (sometimes referred to as Habiru in the literature) were a group of social outcasts, mercenaries, and outlaws that are mentioned in texts of the second millennium BCE from Egypt and the ancient Near East. It is important to note that the term does not denote an ethnic group but a sociological one.

[26]Finkelstein 2007: 18.

[27]Finkelstein 2007: 18.

[28]Mazar 2014: 351.

[29]Mazar 2014: 351.

[30]Mazar 2014: 351.

without ever recovering. This allows us to conclude that the biblical stories that tell us how important Gath was in David's period could very well reflect a reality pertaining to the ninth century BCE and that this is when such stories could have arisen. Be that as it may, the archaeological evidence precludes a date later than the ninth century BCE and therefore once again we are dealing with a phenomenon pertaining to the pre-exilic period.[31]

The Deuteronomistic History (DtrH),[32] that is so well known to biblical scholars, provides us with another case that goes to show that there were pre-exilic traditions current in ancient Israel. Thomas Römer's stance is highly interesting. According to him, the "Deuteronomistic literary production" appears to have started in the seventh century BCE, although "the existence of a Deuteronomistic scribal activity in the time of Josiah does not mean yet that we can trace back to that time the *elaboration* of the Deuteronomistic History in its present form".[33] This latter type of "history" emerged in the exilic period to help the Judaeans to come to terms with the disaster of the exile.[34] Moreover, the DtrH underwent a major redaction in the Persian period when the scrolls of Joshua, Judges, Samuel, and Kings no longer formed part of it, since the scroll of Deuteronomy was joined to the newly constituted Torah, with the result that the DtrH in fact "ceased to exist".[35] It is generally agreed that the DtrH turns out to be a collection of various types of material (either in written form or transmitted orally) that largely dates from before the Babylonian Exile but which was moulded into its current shape mainly during this period.

---

[31]Finkelstein 2007: 18.

[32]The Deuteronomistic History (abbreviated DtrH) consists of the books of Joshua, Judges, Samuel, and Kings, which are considered to have been drawn up largely according to the theological tenets of the book of Deuteronomy, with the latter having originally formed part of the collection but being subsequently included in what is now the Pentateuch.

[33]Römer 2005: 43 (my italics).

[34]Römer 2005: 43.

[35]Römer 2005: 178, see also 181.

However, it is a well-known fact that there are also a number of scholars who do not accept that Israel had historical traditions that date from pre-exilic times,[36] let alone from its proto-historic period spanning approximately from the late thirteenth century BCE to the late tenth century BCE. Archaeology can help us to clarify matters in this regard too, since its results show that the DtrH contains some of the earliest memories of Israel, ones that the writers of the DtrH could not have invented. Such is the case, for example, with the site of Hazor, which Joshua conquered and the king of which he put to the sword; at this point the biblical text tells us that "before that time Hazor was the head of all those kingdoms" (Josh. 11:10). This piece of information is embedded in the DtrH, yet it could not have been invented by the authors of the DtrH since during their time Hazor was of no importance. We have here, therefore, an early memory of Hazor during the second millennium BCE, one that recalls its great status amongst the city states of the southern Levant. Such a status is borne out by a piece of textual information found in Josh. 11:10 as well as the results of the excavations at Hazor. Moreover, it is important to remember that the model of city states each with their own ruler must be an old memory, since when the writers of the DtrH were active this model had long been obsolete.[37]

Archaeological investigation in the southern Levant has also yielded a number of inscriptions that go to show that Israel was definitely a historical entity during the pre-exilic period and that certain biblical texts do relay historical details pertaining to the time from before the Babylonian Exile. Thus, we learn from 2 Kgs 20:20 and 2 Chron. 32:30 that King Hezekiah had channelled the waters of the Gihon spring to a pool inside Jerusalem, namely the pool of Siloam. This feat of engineering is recorded in the well-known Siloam Tunnel inscription that relates how two gangs of workmen

---

[36]For a very radical position on this issue, see Whitelam 1996.
[37]Mazar 2014: 349–50.

(one group working from the north and the other from the south) met.[38] Scholars generally date this inscription to the time of Hezekiah, namely to the eighth century BCE.[39] Yet this was put into question by J. Rogerson and P.R. Davies with the result that the Siloam Inscription could no longer be one clear piece of evidence that there was an Israel before 587/586 BCE; indeed, they preferred to date the inscription to about 550 years later.[40] Ronald S. Hendel immediately rebutted the study by Rogerson and Davies when *inter alia* he made a very detailed palaeographic analysis of the type of scripts prevalent in the Iron Age II and those commonly used in the Hasmonaean period. His detailed study led him to rehabilitate the traditional date and he concluded: "in sum, Rogerson and Davies' conclusions regarding the paleography of the Siloam Inscription are unwarranted. It is possible to distinguish between Iron II and Hasmonean scripts."[41] Furthermore, Hendel succeeded to fit the script employed by the engravers of the Siloam Inscription into the eighth- to seventh-century BCE sequence of scripts.[42] Once again, detailed scholarship won the day since radiocarbon dating on the plaster of the walls on which the inscription was engraved has confirmed the traditional date of the eighth century BCE for the Siloam Inscription, a finding which anchors King Hezekiah and his activities in this century.[43]

A seventh-century BCE letter in Hebrew coming from the fort at Metsad Ḥashavyahu[44] is another piece of epigraphic evidence that shows that the social laws enunciated in Deut. 24:12-13 did not emerge in the post-exilic period, although they are embedded in the DtrH. Indeed, these laws provide

---

[38]Gibson 1971: 21–3.

[39]See, for example, Gibson 1971: 21.

[40]See Rogerson and Davies 1996: 141, where they propose the Hasmonaean period (c. 152–37 BCE) as the "more likely" time when the Siloam Inscription was engraved.

[41]Hendel 1996: 236.

[42]Hendel 1996: 236.

[43]Mazar 2007: 172.

[44]See Naveh 1960.

another clear instance that goes to show that they were not invented by the Deuteronomistic Historians. They were known before the Babylonian Exile and they were the norm in pre-exilic Israel even if they were not yet written in a biblical text that predates this exile. As Mazar writes with respect to the letter from Metsad Ḥashavyahu: "Thus, the Torah laws were well known and utilized in practical life in the seventh century B.C.E.".[45]

Detailed attention to the Hebrew language evidenced both in the Hebrew Bible and in epigraphic Hebrew (unearthed by archaeologists) shows that it is possible to distinguish between pre-exilic and post-exilic Hebrew. A. Hurvitz has provided a solid, clear, and detailed account of how such a distinction can be upheld. The abovementioned Siloam Tunnel inscription and the so-called Lachish Letters[46] (commonly dated respectively to the eighth and the sixth century BCE) are very close to Biblical Hebrew (pre-exilic), whereas Late Biblical Hebrew (post-exilic) is close to the Hebrew of Qumran and to that of the Mishnah.[47] The Hebrew word *spr* is attested both in Biblical Hebrew and in the Lachish Ostraca, where in both it means "letter". In Late Biblical Hebrew (for example in the books of Esther, Nehemiah, and Chronicles) the word *'iggeret* replaces the word *spr*; the same phenomenon often occurs also in Aramaic. According to Hurvitz, "we here have a diachronic development which is manifested within biblical literature in texts belonging to the post-exilic period. Underlying this development is a linguistic process, involving a replacement of the old (classical) *sēper* by its late (post-classical) counterpart *'iggeret*."[48]

---

[45]Mazar 2007b: 179.

[46]Torczyner 1938. In fact, not all the inscribed potsherds in question are letters, and it is preferable to refer to them as the Lachish Ostraca as scholars commonly do nowadays. For a thorough discussion of this matter see Zammit 2016.

[47]Hurvitz 1997, see especially pp. 308–11.

[48]Hurvitz 1997: 312.

Recently, in a very detailed linguistic study titled "Diachronic Linguistics and the Date of the Pentateuch", J. Joosten has confirmed and indeed refined even further the results that Hurvitz had reached.[49] Joosten has shown beyond any reasonable doubt that when all the evidence is taken into consideration we cannot but uphold a distinction between Classical and Late Biblical Hebrew. He is very much aware that this distinction could be rather rough and not that refined. Nevertheless, historical linguistics does allow us to maintain that there are biblical texts written in Hebrew that originated from before the Babylonian Exile in distinction to others stemming from the fifth century BCE or even later. As he says, "to extend the period of creative writing in CBH [Classical Biblical Hebrew] to the fifth century or later means taking the approach beyond the breaking point. Dating a text like Gen 12:10-20 to the late Persian period can only be done if its language is left out of consideration."[50] Obviously, for a scholar to ignore some of the available evidence would not be the right thing to do.

The foregoing examples mentioned and discussed in a rather summary fashion are meant as tasters of what is involved when one decides to approach Biblical Archaeology. By now it will have become clear that the aims that I would like to reach in this book and which were already outlined above can only be achieved if we really go back to the basics, to the nuts and bolts, both of archaeology as well as of the fundamental principles involved when integrating the results of biblical and archaeological research. Indeed, to be *critically* aware of the results of the archaeology of the ancient Near East, especially of the southern Levant, is indispensable; no scholar would consider this as being a luxury. As already shown above, often it is archaeology that

---

[49]Joosten 2016: 330, where with reference to the substitution of the word *sēper* with *'iggeret*, he writes: "The replacement had the added advantage of eliminating the ambiguity arising from the use of *sēper*, which could refer to all kinds of written documents, in particular books. The conclusion must be that *sēper* in the meaning "letter" is an earlier word and *'iggeret* a later one." (My transliterations replace Hebrew characters in the foregoing quote.)
[50]Joosten 2016: 344.

comes to our rescue when deciding crucial matters such as whether there ever really was a pre-exilic Israel and a pre-exilic type of Hebrew. In the process, as shown by the examples discussed thus far, the close attention to minute details is essential. Before proceeding further, it is time to have a look at what archaeology is really all about.

2

What did the excavators actually find? The archaeological data and their interpretation

The examples discussed in the previous chapter make it clear that we now have to turn our attention to the basics of archaeology in order for biblical scholars to appreciate what is involved in the critical assessment of the archaeological reports that they encounter in their research when attempting to integrate the results of archaeological investigations with those of biblical scholarship. It is clear that the first thing to look at is the discipline of archaeology itself.

What is archaeology? The books on archaeology as a discipline are legion[1] and its definitions vary (at least somewhat) from one publication to the other. Thus it is worthwhile to pin down the common factors that go

---

[1]Here I single out three books. For one of the latest up-to-date and comprehensive introductions to archaeology in general see Renfrew and Bahn 2016. Kenyon 1961, though somewhat outdated on the application of scientific methods to archaeology, is superb as an introduction to the basics of archaeological excavation and the essential thought processes of archaeologists. Finally, Shafer-Elliott 2016 is an excellent springboard from which to dive into the archaeology of the southern Levant, and thus it is ideal for biblical scholars.

to make up the essential hallmarks of this vast field in order to provide a definition that is sufficiently comprehensive. I would define archaeology as the methodical retrieval (very often by excavation) and study of the material remains of past human societies with a view to reconstructing the story of our ancestors (including that of their culture and behaviour). One could argue as to where the boundaries of "past" really lie, since strictly speaking the moment something has gone by it belongs to the past. So, as such, midnight yesterday could turn out to be a good cut-off point for the *terminus ante quem* for archaeological research. However there is no need to quibble about this point since on reflection it becomes clear that archaeology is in fact linked to history. As I have already written elsewhere, in his book titled *Archaeology from the Earth* Sir Mortimer Wheeler[2] explains "the techniques of field archaeology showing how we can reliably extract information from the ground that is needed to reconstruct the overall story of our ancestors, including that which took place during that very long stretch of time predating the invention of writing c. 3500 B.C.".[3] Hence, we should not be surprised when we read that archaeology can be considered as a "specialized form of history"[4] or that there are books with titles such as *History from the Earth: An Introduction to Archaeology*.[5] Indeed, archaeologists purport to tell the story of humankind, and those whom we call (via a misnomer) prehistorians are "prehistorians by necessity, not by choice".[6] It is important to remember that all material remains unearthed in excavation, be they written or not, do constitute the object of archaeological research.

The foregoing points underscore the fact that "as for archaeology, if it cannot write *some* kind of history, it will be reduced to mere antiquarianism".[7]

---

[2]Wheeler 1954.
[3]Frendo 2015: 217.
[4]Woodhead 1985: 10.
[5]Forde-Johnston 1974.
[6]Grabbe 1997: 22.
[7]Dever 2003: 521.

There was a time in the recent history of archaeology when the guns of many were turned against this viewpoint, "but today's postprocessual approaches have brought us back full circle to archaeology as a basically historical discipline".[8] In this sense it is a pity to register the fact that relatively few archaeologists state *clearly* that archaeology does include inscriptions as one of its data sets, since it is important to remember that they too are written *material* remains. It therefore comes as a relief to read that "the archaeology of ancient civilisations often includes the study of inscriptions and ancient languages. This is especially true of Egyptology, Assyriology, and Mayan archaeology."[9] The corollary of all this is that we have a more complete, and thus better, access to the story of our ancestors by integrating the disciplines of archaeology and history. When studying those periods for which written evidence is available, we are duty bound to integrate in a sound methodological manner the unwritten as well as the written evidence, whether the latter stems from archaeological research or not.[10]

What is the nature of archaeological evidence? To start with, we do well to remove from our minds the idea of glamour and grandeur when it comes to archaeological data. Monuments like the pyramids of Egypt or the Colosseum in Rome are the exception and not the rule. More often than not, archaeologists leave large "holes" in the ground after they finish excavating an area, since in order to get to the remains left by our ancestors that lie in the deeper levels of a site they must destroy the evidence as they go down, which in turn means that they must record well all their finds (including objects and layers of soil). Short of this, the data will be lost; indeed, the archaeological data (except for the site and its landscape) are found in the field notes and only in a second instance are they relayed in the archaeological reports, in museums,

---

[8]Dever 2003: 520.
[9]Henson 2012: 84.
[10]For the integration of textual and unwritten evidence, see Frendo 2011: 26–38, and especially see also de Vaux 1970. Still highly noteworthy is the study by Dymond (1974).

and nowadays often also on the World Wide Web. Only if the recording in the field is done properly will the archaeological reports and all the other places relaying the archaeological data be deemed reliable.

More often than not, archaeologists retrieve broken artefacts; indeed, they find lots of pottery sherds, stumps of walls, rubbish in pits, innumerable layers of soil, and such like material. This is what had led A.R. Millard to view archaeological evidence as random and fragmentary.[11] Since such is the case, then archaeologists can only go by what they find, and it would be a flawed and fallacious argument to draw positive conclusions from the absence of evidence. In other words, if we do not encounter a certain phenomenon on a site it does not mean that that phenomenon never existed or took place. Thus, for example, "every adult knows that on Ground Zero in southern Manhattan in New York there had once stood the mighty Twin Towers which were annihilated on September 11th 2001. However, hardly any material evidence survived to allow any archaeologist to reconstruct what there had once actually been."[12] Indeed, out of 2,752 victims there was a "devastating gap left by the complete vaporization of nearly 2,000 people".[13] In simple terms, this means that there was no archaeological evidence for the magnitude of the disaster that had hit the Twin Towers, and had this lack of evidence been the only thing to go by, *some* archaeologists could have erroneously concluded that any document that recorded this major disaster would have simply fabricated this tragic event. It would all have been a fiction without reference to reality. But clearly such is not the case, and biblical scholars can readily understand how fallacious the argument from silence is; indeed, mutatis mutandis such a scenario reminds us of those cases when certain biblical events and personages (or their deeds) are relegated by some scholars to the realm of fiction simply because no corroborating archaeological evidence

[11]Millard 1991a: 21.
[12]Frendo 2011: 31.
[13]Wallace 2004: 149; see also 148.

for them was found. Such, for example, is the case of the ascription of the Jerusalem temple to Solomon. There is no archaeological evidence to prove that King Solomon built this temple, but this lack of evidence does not mean that he did not. Indeed, "it is tempting to add that it would be strange if the temple came only subsequently and erroneously to be ascribed to Solomon, since such an institution is not likely to have had its origins manipulated, but for that supposition there is no external evidence".[14]

As pointed out above, the recording of the data is crucial, and it is important to remember that there is a distinction between the data and our interpretation of them. Indeed, one can readily understand that, as already discussed in Chapter 1, an ash layer can turn out to be the result either of a violent destruction or of a domestic fire, and a conclusion can only be reached once the context is taken into account.[15] It is important to know whether the ash in question was caused by a destructive fire or is the residue of some other kind of burning (combustion for cooking or heating, for example), since this would impact on our story of a given area. If a conflagration can be identified, we might then move on to analysing whether a site was destroyed by some enemy or by an accidental fire. This simple example shows us that the data are not identical to truth, or knowledge, and that to reach the latter we first need to understand the available data.[16] However, our insight, or understanding of the data, has to be verified against the data themselves, it has to be checked with the evidence. As I pointed out elsewhere, "A judgment must be made as to whether there is sufficient evidence for a statement to be maintained or not. Thus, the human mind turns out as having a dynamic cognitional structure which passes through three stages: data, insight, and judgment".[17]

---

[14]Williamson 2015.

[15]Brandfon 1987: 33, 34.

[16]Elsewhere I have discussed at more length the issue of how we come to know the past and whether it is at all possible to do so; see Frendo 2011: 52–60 and Frendo 2003.

[17]Frendo 2011: 57 and references there.

The foregoing points imply clearly that, if our recording of the data is flawed (such as by the presentation of unclear photographs, and/or unsatisfactory drawings of the objects retrieved, including the ground plans and sections of the layers and architectural remains), then it follows that our interpretation of the data is doomed to failure with the result that we shall never know what the archaeologists had really found. This is precisely the point: we need to know what was actually found on a site, and we can only succeed in doing this if the archaeologists present the data to us clearly, without obfuscating them with their own interpretations which could be incorrect. We need to check the statements and the stories that archaeologists narrate to us against the data that they themselves present to us. In other words, archaeologists owe us good archaeological reports.

This latter point is important and it leads us to ask a simple but crucial question: What is a report? A report is the presentation of the data (in the form of words, and by illustration where applicable) in a clear and precise manner, keeping separate *as much as is humanly possible* the interpretation of the data from the latter themselves. This means that in report writing archaeologists have to concentrate on the *presentation* of the data keeping their interpretation of the latter to the barest minimum. I say this because the report has to allow readers to check the interpretation of the excavators against the data that the former themselves present. In other words, a report has to be largely descriptive. However, I wrote "*as much as is humanly possible*" with reference to keeping separate the data from their interpretation, because in truth there is no such thing as a pure description—the latter implies a modicum of interpretation since when we approach and experience the data we do not do so with an "empty head".[18] On the contrary, we come to the data with our own thoughts, ideas, preconceptions, world view and so on, and our understanding of the data will be emended via the "self-correcting

---

[18]Lonergan 1973: 157.

process of learning"[19] which in its own turn allows us to see the data for what they are. Indeed, as I have noted elsewhere, "The human mind attains fact by passing through the 'self-correcting process of learning'[20] in such a way that the original assumptions themselves are duly scrutinized before facts are established".[21] It is only because things are so that one can decide whether the ash layer discussed above and in Chapter 1 is the result of a domestic burning or some more general destructive fire event. However since in a report one is obliged to keep the data distinct from their interpretation "*as much as is humanly possible*", it is clear that the right thing to do is to describe the layer in question in the first instance simply as "an ash layer" and only thereafter to decide whether it is due to a domestic fire or to a violent destruction. In this manner the reader of archaeological reports can check the excavators' interpretation against the data that the latter present clearly, and within the overall context, thereby possibly reaching a different conclusion to that of the excavators. A good archaeological report allows the reader to reach a conclusion as to what was actually found, and this may be different to what the excavators themselves surmised. On the contrary, an archaeological report that is not up to standard forces the reader to believe the interpretation of the finds given by the excavators.

In this context it is interesting to note that when discussing the notion of the archaeological record Ian Hodder makes a contrast between the attitude and practice of General Pitt-Rivers and that of Sir Flinders Petrie. The former recorded everything in great detail so that subsequent investigators would be able to concentrate on aspects of a given site that were not of immediate interest to the original excavators. In the process of recording and presenting the data, personal opinions were kept to a bare minimum.[22] In contrast,

---

[19]Lonergan 1973: 159.
[20]A phrase used by Lonergan 1973: 159.
[21]Frendo 2011: 58 and references there.
[22]Hodder 1999: 22 and references there.

regarding Petrie's approach to presenting the data, Hodder writes, "it is at least sadly true that he does not find anything he does not look for".[23] The clear presentation of the data is crucial since archaeology purports to be one very important gateway to the past. And yet things tend to become more complicated still when we consider that the archaeological record itself is not a straightforward relic from the past. Indeed, as Linda E. Patrik states with reference to Michael B. Schiffer's stance regarding the nature of the archaeo-logical record, we must not forget that "in many cases, these [archaeological] remains have been altered by natural and cultural processes between the time they were output materials, deposited by a past cultural system, and the time that they are excavated and 'read' as a record by archaeologists".[24] I find myself in agreement with Hodder when he states that "some interpretation is involved in the most descriptive statements,"[25] that is, on condition that in the first instance the interpretation is kept to a bare minimum. This can only be achieved if we realize that "interpretation is always interpretation of something. Thus it is always partially a description."[26]

Hodder goes on to tell us that the natural world, books, and human activity are all "texts" which need to be read and that "in all areas of discovery, the data are never entirely objective or simply 'given'".[27] However, this statement needs to be qualified somewhat since it is important to also keep in mind the fact that objectivity is not linked to the data, but to the judgement that we make after verifying our understanding of the data against the data

---

[23]Hodder 1999: 22 and references there.

[24]Patrik 1985: 50 and references there.

[25]Hodder 1999: 68. The example that Hodder gives is that of making use of "codified soil descriptions". He notes that when attempting to answer the question as to whether the soil we have at hand is gritty or not, our answer is bound to have an element of subjectivity in it (Hodder 1999: 67–8). While this is true, we can get out of this impasse and remain objective if we remember that the "self-correcting process of learning" discussed above in Chapter 1 is what guarantees that we ensure that we are objective in our understanding of the data. Indeed, "genuine objectivity is the fruit of authentic subjectivity" (Lonergan 1973: 292).

[26]Hodder 1999: 67.

[27]Hodder 1999: 32.

themselves. As Bernard J.F. Lonergan writes with respect to a text that an interpreter handles, what the latter sees are "just a series of signs"; in fact, "anything over and above a reissue of the same signs in the same order will be mediated by the experience, intelligence, and judgement of the interpreter. The less that experience, the less cultivated that intelligence, the less formed that judgement, the greater the likelihood that the interpreter will impute to the author an opinion that the author never entertained."[28] The same holds good for archaeology; the data, the "signs out there", have to be understood and our insight has to be verified by going back to the data in order to see whether our understanding of them, our conclusions, are true or not. I have dwelt somewhat at length on *how* archaeologists reach their conclusions since, unfortunately, this topic is often ignored in the archaeological literature; it is true to say that "of course, much has been written on method—how archaeologists dig, label, analyse. But little has been published on how archaeologists decide that they have reached a satisfactory interpretation."[29]

When it comes to Biblical Archaeology, it is really important to keep in mind the aforementioned points about how archaeologists reach the conclusions on which they base their respective stories of our ancestors. It goes without saying that the Bible deals with sacred space, and there is no doubt that the biblical authors "knew the narratives that linked mythic with geographical space. They knew; we do not."[30] Thus, we need to examine very carefully all the available data before we can reach satisfactory conclusions. It is not always clear how archaeologists of the southern Levant have reached their conclusions regarding the cultic function of certain artefacts that they excavate. Such, for example, is the case with incense burners. It is interesting to note that Seymour Gitin studied the form and function of the four-horned altars, concluding that they were used as incense burners and that they therefore

[28]Lonergan 1973: 157.
[29]Hodder 1999: 20 and references there.
[30]Zevit 2002: 81.

had a cultic function. Such "four-horned altars" used as incense burners were actually found both in industrial and domestic quarters, with the inevitable result that archaeologists had to rethink the term "sacred space". Indeed, with respect to thirteen such four-horned altars from Ekron, "the olive oil industrial and domestic zones of occupation" where these altars were found go to show, so the theory goes, that such find spots can be considered as "sacred spaces" because of "the presence of a sacred object used for a cultic purpose— that is the burning of incense".[31] But is this really so? Do the data support such a conclusion and the story that one could narrate on its basis? The evidence does not seem to support Gitin's conclusion if we think very carefully and if we keep in mind that the burning of incense per se is not necessarily to be identified as a cultic act. Indeed, people in antiquity could have very well burnt incense for reasons unrelated to religious worship, as a deodorant or "air freshener". Moreover, the four-horned altars could have been used as braziers.[32] As such, it does not follow that an incense burner (and there is nothing to stop the four-horned altars being identified as such) in isolation means that we are dealing with a cultic artefact—this might be the case, but it is not necessarily so. This is one clear example of how biblical scholars should critically evaluate the reports, news, and information that archaeologists provide them with. The point is that we should always consider very carefully what the archaeologists have really unearthed. The overriding question should be: *What did the excavators actually find?* The process involved in answering such a question is the exercise of our dynamic powers of human cognition, discussed above, for "no matter what its field of research happens to be, the human mind starts out with some inevitable assumption or theory and studies the available data with a view to understanding them. However, this is not sufficient for it to reach the truth; in order to do this it must check whether its own insight is correct, and if it turns out to be so, then truth is reached. A judgement must be made

---

[31]Gitin 2002: 113; see also 112, 115–17.
[32]Fowler 1984: 184–5.

as to whether there is sufficient evidence for a statement to be maintained or not."[33] Such an exercise of our inbuilt cognitional structure will help protect us against any type of "unfounded speculation".[34]

Another example of how careful we must be in distinguishing between the archaeological data and interpretations offered by the excavators is the case of the so-called copper smelting industry at Tell el-Kheleifeh, allegedly dating to the tenth century BCE and which had been commonly linked with King Solomon. Nelson Glueck, the excavator of the site between 1938 and 1940, interpreted the archaeological data, concluding that he had found at this site Solomon's copper smelting industry. He claimed to have found a number of features and artefacts that supported his conclusions: flue holes, hand bellows, clay crucibles, and furnace remains. Revisiting the data, Israel Finkelstein concluded that a closer look at the data reveals that the "flue holes" can be easily viewed as holes used to support wooden beams, whereas the "clay crucibles" turn out to be "sherds of locally produced, handmade pottery vessels". Moreover, there were in fact "only a few metallic finds" found by Glueck at Tell el-Kheleifeh.[35] Yet the argument that really dismantles the original story and which goes to show that Solomon could not have had a copper smelting industry at Tell el-Kheleifeh is that it was subsequently shown that this site was founded only in the late eighth/early seventh century BCE.[36] This example goes to show that "the inherent motivation of the archaeologist to expose physical and tangible data, with the goal of producing a scientific analysis of the finds and an unbiased presentation of data and results, has proven elusive. Archaeological evidence per se is always partial and contaminated, and our knowledge, regardless of how meticulous and comprehensive our investigation, relies primarily on extrapolation, interpretation, and

[33]Frendo 2011: 57.
[34]Pitard 2002: 163.
[35]Finkelstein 2007: 11.
[36]Finkelstein 2007: 11.

imagination."[37] However, as the discussion later in this chapter will show, it is possible to reach conclusions that are reliable on condition that we re-examine the data more carefully, especially by exercising the above-mentioned "self-correcting process of learning". It is clear that to reach correct conclusions does not mean that there is nothing further to investigate; we have to distinguish between conclusions that are false, and those that are true but partial and that will be enhanced by further inquiry.

A classic example of how the archaeological data can be misread is that of the archaeological misidentification of the biblical *bāmāh*, commonly rendered as "high place" in many English versions of the Hebrew Bible. I shall deal with this topic in more depth in Chapter 5. However, I would like to mention this example here in order to show how the above-mentioned "self-correcting process of learning" helps us to identify our errors and to reach satisfactory answers once we do our best to see whether the data really support our statements or not. It will be shown in Chapter 5 that there are problems even at the philological level as to what a *bāmāh* really denotes in the Hebrew Bible, and this makes it difficult for archaeologists to pin down with certainty a *bāmāh* in their excavations. Indeed, we can truly say that "given our present very incomplete knowledge of what a bamah really was and looked like, we need to find an edifice actually labelled 'bamah' before we can be sure".[38]

At Petra there were the remains of a monument that had originally been "read" as a *bāmāh* on a site known as "The Conway High Place". Peter J. Parr went back to the archaeological data and checked them very carefully. Parr's results show that in reality the so-called Conway High Place consisted of three main elements: a rock outcrop, two trenches (A and B) cut into the rock, and a wall (C) encircling these two trenches. This structure was positioned at a

---

[37]Galor 2017: 4.
[38]Ap-Thomas 1975: 167.

location that afforded an excellent view of the city, though the structure itself was not visible from below. To the south-west of wall C there was also a small platform on which there was an altar and a moulded pedestal.[39] Thanks to Parr's accurate observations we know that the platform, and consequently the altar and the moulded pedestal, *postdate* wall C. Hence, there is no necessary link whatsoever between the clearly religious nature of the altar and the pedestal, and the original purpose and role of the monument.[40] On the basis of the aforementioned points, which are the result of Parr's detailed stratigraphic analysis, it is highly probable that "Conway's High Place" would be better termed "Conway's Round Tower".[41] In fact, wall A turns out to be a massive round tower that formed part of a military fortification, one wall of which was wall C. Originally this latter wall had been interpreted as a processional way linked to the "high place", but this is highly imaginative since the surface of C would not have been at all comfortable for a procession![42] The overall picture of the monument that Parr correctly interprets as a fortification rather than as a "high place" consists of the following: a circular tower (= A and B) that C expanded and encircled, to the west and south of which there were remnants of walls.[43]

Parr does not provide a precise date for the Round Tower, but he does point out that the pottery and coins indicate that the Round Tower was likely used as a fortification towards the end of the first century BCE/beginning of the first century CE. It is interesting to note that the aforementioned wall to the west of wall C was niched and thus of a Hellenistic type. In the following centuries the tower was abandoned and eventually came to be located *outside* the city walls in an area used as a cemetery—hence the votive type of pottery

[39]Parr 1962: 67–9.
[40]Parr 1962: 69, 72.
[41]Parr 1962: 74.
[42]Parr 1962: 71–2.
[43]Parr 1962, Pl. I; 75.

that was retrieved. In historical terms, the tower of Petra had shrunk in importance when Rome annexed it in 106 CE.[44] My point here, once again, is that a careful re-examination of the data leads to reinterpretation: in this case the "Conway High Place" is no *bāmāh* at all but a fortification structure that eventually lost its defensive role.

As already discussed above, the evidence that archaeology yields is random and fragmentary. This makes it quite difficult to get a clear picture of the past and that is why archaeology is only one gateway—though a very important one, of course—into antiquity. Archaeologists present certain information and stories of the past to biblical scholars, specialists who have to take these results on board in their interpretation of the relevant biblical texts. However, it is crucial for biblical scholars to first be aware of their own cognitional structure in order to be able to ascertain what archaeologists really find; they need to verify the statements and conclusions against the data in an attempt to get at what was really found on a site. The foregoing examples, all of which interact with the Bible in some way or another, illustrate this.

However, before discussing the relationship between written and non-written evidence, I would like to give a striking example—this time not from the field of Biblical Archaeology—of the distinction between the data and the original interpretation of the excavators in order to illustrate the importance of our question: "What did the excavators actually find?" Importantly, it takes understanding and the verification of our own insights to appreciate what data we are really dealing with.

Detected under the water off the Greek island of Zakynthos, snorkelers and divers had detected what they took to be "ruins" in the subtidal waters not far from the shore of the Ionian island of Zakynthos. The remains appeared to be of a submerged city, possibly of the Hellenic Age. The structures took the forms of slabs and columns, though they were not accompanied by "any

---

[44]Parr 1962: 75–7.

further supporting evidence for antiquities at this site". The oddity led a team of researchers to look into the possibility of a geological origin for these remains.[45] Their hunch was confirmed when the researchers concluded that the "remains" of the alleged Hellenic city turned out to be natural geological concretions, "fossil features possibly of Pliocene age based on Sr isotope data".[46]

This is a clear instance of how important it is to critically assess the archaeological reports we encounter. The underwater "remains" of the alleged Hellenic city off the shore of the island of Zakynthos turned out to be neither those of a city nor of the Hellenic Age! The original interpretation did not stand the test of verification. What was actually discovered were the remains of very ancient natural geological processes and not traces of human activity. A reconsideration of the data brought about a complete rethink of the nature and dating of the site.

This example hopefully goes to show that *critical* consciousness is invaluable when approaching archaeological information. Indeed, as J.E. Andrews and his co-researchers wrote: "We summarise our findings with the maxim 'all that glistens is not gold' or in this case 'columns and pavements in the sea, not always antiquities will be'".[47] The same rule of thumb applies to Biblical Archaeology.

[45] Andrews et al. 2016: 16.
[46] Andrews et al. 2016: 24.
[47] Andrews et al. 2016: 16.

3
Artefacts:
Inscribed and uninscribed

The points made in the previous chapter illustrate that biblical scholars should critically assess the reports that archaeologists hand over to them in order to find out what the latter have really discovered. Doing this, biblical scholars will be in a much better position to undertake the next crucial step, namely that of integrating the results of the archaeologists with those of their own biblical research. This integration is possible, on condition that in the first instance both the archaeological and the biblical research are undertaken separately according to their own rules and methods of operation.[1] Archaeologists are bound to operate as if there were no biblical data, whilst biblical scholars have to study the biblical texts according to the rules pertaining to their field and as if there were no archaeological research. Only thereafter may scholars compare and contrast the results of the biblical investigation with the archaeological one. It is only then that one can speak of Biblical Archaeology, and only at this point that the Bible can throw light on the results of archaeology and vice versa depending on the particular case. When archaeology and biblical

[1] De Vaux 1970: 70.

research are brought together it is clear that the scholars involved, and not only the archaeologists, find themselves dealing with artefacts.

But what is an artefact? Timothy Darvill aptly defines an artefact as "any object which has been modified, fashioned, or manufactured according to a set of humanly imposed attributes, including tools, weapons, ornaments, utensils, houses, buildings, etc. Artefacts are the basic components of MATERIAL CULTURE."[2] According to this definition both the Bible and ancient inscriptions retrieved in archaeological excavations qualify as artefacts since they are both the product of human activity. Indeed, when it comes to the Bible one should consider that it too is an artefact. If an artefact can be thought of as an item held in a library or museum, we can bring to mind the Leningrad Codex, the oldest extant complete copy of the Hebrew Bible. Or if an artefact is defined as an item unearthed through archaeological exploration, the ancient copies of the Hebrew Bible found amongst the Qumran Scrolls should be so identified. It is clear that the term "artefact" should not be restricted to archaeological finds alone.

It is customary to classify textual material as being either literary or archaeological. So, for example, it is a commonplace that the copies of the Bible held in libraries from generation to generation are deemed to be literary works, whilst copies of the same text that are retrieved in archaeological excavations are viewed as archaeological artefacts. Indeed, in this latter case some scholars also distinguish between palaeography and epigraphy depending on whether one is dealing with writing found respectively on papyri or on hard materials.[3]

---

[2]Darvill 2002: 25.

[3]Healey 1990: 14. However, as Healey himself points out, this distinction turns out to be "artificial" since both epigraphy and palaeography "are part and parcel of a community's 'epigraphic' remains. In relation to Semitic inscriptions [and thus Semitic epigraphy], it is common to use the term palaeography for a particular aspect of the study of writing on all materials, i.e. the study of the progressive developments and changes in the forms of letters or signs" (Healey 1990: 14). In this sense we could therefore speak of the palaeography of inscriptions. Scholars use the typology of letter forms as an aid to dating in view of the fact that they trace the developments of these types over time. Clearly this approach can only produce rough estimates of dates, since old letter forms can remain in use in

If we reflect very carefully on these issues, however, it soon becomes clear that the nomenclature in current use leads us to an impasse. I have in mind the case of the *Epic of Gilgamesh* which is viewed as one of the earliest (if not the earliest) pieces of great literature, but which is also clearly an archaeological artefact seeing that it was incised on clay tablets that were retrieved in archaeological investigations.[4] In other words, the *Epic of Gilgamesh* is at one and the same time a literary and an archaeological product. So, what are we to do? I think that it would be better to use a simpler and at the same time a more comprehensive type of terminology. Rather than grouping archaeological artefacts into non-literary texts and "archaeological finds of other kinds [such as architectural]",[5] I think that it is preferable to simply speak of inscribed and uninscribed artefacts. Indeed, this distinction can be applied to all artefacts whether they are archaeological or not. Such a typology of artefacts would allow one to include in the archaeological repertoire textual material retrieved in archaeological excavations that is at the same time very literary in nature, as in the case of the *Epic of Gilgamesh* just mentioned. Moreover, since, as shown above, artefacts are not only those items retrieved during excavations, this typology of dividing all human artefacts into inscribed and uninscribed allows for a smoother integration of all the relevant written material with that which is not. In the case of the Bible, this means that scholars not only can, but are (by the nature of the evidence) obliged, to integrate all the relevant written evidence with that which is unwritten, whether retrieved in archaeological investigations or not.

The upshot of the foregoing proposal is that written evidence can be wholly integrated in archaeology and that it would really form part and parcel of it, thus leading to a more holistic view of the past. Such a holistic approach can

later periods in some areas but not in others. Moreover, the dating of the various types of letters in turn depends on dates that are available via various dating techniques such as the ones discussed in Chapter 4.

[4] A. George 2003a: xv.

[5] Horsley 1992: 164.

help us to redress somewhat the random and fragmentary nature of archae-ology[6] as well as the "inevitably fragmentary nature of the information and the distorting effects of narrative structuring"[7] that we encounter in accounts about the human past. It is clear that the study of documents (whether found in archaeological investigations or not) and that of uninscribed artefacts (whether unearthed in archaeological excavations or not) can benefit us greatly if we integrate all the pertinent results. Only by carefully juxtaposing one discipline with the other—after having carefully examined the relevant data according to their specific rules of interpretation—can we hope to overcome the random and fragmentary nature of archaeology and the selective and distorted picture of the past gained through the study of the relevant texts.

Some scholars claim that, since archaeology is not linked with our memory of the past, it can represent that past more faithfully than written records do.[8] However, there are two things to note in this regard. The first is that it is true that "memory is an unreliable servant",[9] and that therefore only after examining their documents critically can historians access the past. The second point to consider is that, although archaeologists bypass memory[10] and have direct access to the data from the past, still these data need first to be understood and the relative insights that scholars make must be verified before the archaeologists can draw any solid conclusions about the past.[11] Indeed, the nature of historical and archaeological evidence is much more similar than is commonly thought. Just as history can only be accessed

---

[6]Millard 1991a: 21.

[7]Kuhrt 2000: 258.

[8]Brandfon 1987: 8.

[9]Sertillanges 1987: 186.

[10]Still, as already discussed above, the very fact that archaeological evidence is both random and fragmentary is tantamount to there being an "archaeological" (Brandfon 1987: 10) memory that clearly does not give us the whole picture of the past. In this sense, both history and archaeology depend on memory, which does not represent the whole past.

[11]Frendo 2011: 52–60, especially 57–8; see also Frendo 2003: 607–8.

through historiography, so the archaeological record can only be reached through the archaeological reports. In fact, "the archaeological record is, finally the documents that describe what was recovered and analyzed and what procedures were used".[12] This is precisely why, when it comes to archaeology, we always have to ask ourselves the question "What did the excavators actually find?", as already discussed in the previous chapter. Similarly, when we read texts (such as those of the Bible) we have to realize that we can reach historical reconstructions only by attending critically to the texts (the equivalent of an archaeological report) before us. As John Barton states, "critics initially attended to the text just as it lay before them. But when they attempted to read it just as it lay before them, they noticed inconsistencies: inconsistencies, that is, within the text *as it stands*."[13] Thus biblical scholars can reconstruct the past (to which the Bible often refers) more faithfully and precisely, only after reading critically the reports of archaeologists as well as the written documents relative to their topic of research and then integrate the results of each exercise.

It is apparent that both in archaeological as well as in historical research scholars are the ones who reconstruct the story of past human beings. They do this by examining carefully the archaeological history of ancient sites as well as by narrating the story of past human beings on the basis of a critical reading of ancient documents. In effect, they have to draw a picture of the past based on "unrelated pieces of evidence".[14] Bob Becking has used this phrase with reference to things like names and legal customs, which "cannot be classified as history"[15] and which confront scholars after the latter have peeled off even the ideology contained in an original source or layer of a narrative. Such a scenario is parallel to what obtains in archaeology, which

[12]Schiffer 1987: 339.
[13]Barton 2000: 36.
[14]Becking 2000: 132.
[15]Becking 2000: 132.

is also characterised by the accumulation of "unrelated pieces of evidence" that scholars join together. It is incumbent on archaeologists to understand the data they excavate and to verify whether their understanding stands the rigour of verification in the light of the overall context of the sites under examination. Becking avoids the pitfalls of positivistic thinking in historical research. The example he gives is taken from a narrative in 1 Kings 21 that clearly contains a Deuteronomistic layer. When this layer (vv. 20, 21, 25, and 26) is removed we are left with the original story, which, however, "is still a narrative text that gives a selection and a reorganization of elements of the events that supposedly have taken place".[16]

The foregoing paragraphs show clearly that the study of all human artefacts is the basis for reconstructing the story of our ancestors. All artefacts (whether inscribed or not and whether they are retrieved in archaeological research or not) pertinent to a given research question should first be studied on their own merits and only secondarily can scholars integrate all the relevant results in order to reconstruct the human past. To achieve this integration in a healthy manner without doing any violence to the evidence there are a number of important things that need to be kept in mind. J. Nicholas Postgate reminds scholars that to link general archaeological research with written evidence it is imperative to avoid drawing conclusions from the absence of evidence. He also criticizes the reckless use of words and assumptions,[17] and he points out that one should avoid making sweeping statements "without the necessary 'perhaps' or substantiation", using circular arguments, and trans-forming one's theory into fact. He also deplores the use of a dosage of theory "unfamiliar to the philologist".[18]

[16]Becking 2000: 132.
[17]Postgate 1990: 235–6.
[18]Postgate 1990: 238.

In order to achieve a healthy marriage between scholars' interpretations of both the written and unwritten data, it is important to first understand the texts in question well—indeed, this is crucial. Without a good, initial understanding of the texts we would run the risk of imposing a theoretical model on the written sources rather than using our models to explain things clearly. Thus, for example, with reference to the study of the New Testament, G.H.R. Horsley wrote: "linguistic skills are an essential undergirding to ensure that the texts are not being misread or misapprehended historically when theoretical models are being tested out on them".[19] This applies equally well to the study of the Hebrew Bible, and to the field of Biblical Archaeology. Indeed, not only the biblical text but also inscribed artefacts are very important when it comes to reconstructing the past human history to which the Bible refers. As M.D. Coogan aptly wrote with reference to the identity of Early Israel: "in the absence of determinative written evidence, it is impossible in the early Iron Age to identify a particular artifact, script, house, feature, or site as Israelite".[20] The essential role of understanding correctly the written evidence within the context of integrating written with unwritten evidence can also be seen when one considers the "standing stones" (the *maṣṣēbôt* of the Hebrew Bible) mentioned in various biblical texts. The *maṣṣēbôt* were used in several different contexts, the primary one being that of commemoration. But one would like to know which type of commemoration the texts are referring to. It could just as easily be a funerary or a cultic one, although generally it was a funerary type of commemoration during which the *maṣṣēbôt* were set upright (see Gen. 35:19-20; 2 Sam. 18:18). It would be extremely difficult to glean such precise information purely from the unwritten material evidence.[21]

---

[19]Horsley 1992: 164.

[20]Coogan 1987: 6. In the southern Levant, national cultures emerge only towards the end of the early Iron Age; up to that point "it would be wise to avoid labels such as Israelite or Canaanite unless there is conclusive evidence for using them" (Coogan 1987: 6).

[21]Lewis 2002: 179.

There are times when two different inscriptions retrieved in archaeological investigations can throw light on each other, as well as on the Bible.
Thus, for example, the inscription known as the "Kurkh Monolith"[22] "lists
'two thousand chariots' for the army of Ahab the Israelite, which is exactly
the amount of chariots mentioned by Hazael in the Dan Stela".[23] This means
that the Kurkh Monolith very probably included the chariots from Judah in
its overall estimation—an exact parallel to what Hazael did in the inscribed
stela from Tel Dan. Hazael also claims that he killed Joram of Israel as well
as Achazyahu of Judah. However, this claim runs counter to what we find in
2 Kgs 9:1–10:28, where we read that it was Jehu who killed these two kings
during his coup. Who actually killed Joram and Achazyahu? Was it Hazael, as
we read in the Tel Dan Stela, or was it Jehu, as we are told in 2 Kgs 9:1–10:28?[24]
This latter source is "probably close to the event"[25] whereas it is likely that
the Tel Dan Stela was inscribed about twenty to thirty years later, making
it likely that in this case the biblical source is the one that is more reliable.
This is not the only case in documents from the ancient Near East dating to
the ninth century BCE where we find that two leaders both claim credit for
the same action. Thus, the aforementioned Kurkh Monument reports that
nobles had killed Giammu, their lord. However, fifteen years later we find that
Shalmaneser III claims in an inscription on a marble slab that he had been the
one to kill Giammu. Once again, it is highly probable that the source closer

---

[22]The Kurkh Monolith is a large stela of stone that has inscribed on it one version of the annals of
Shalmaneser III. It ends abruptly just after mentioning the battle of Qarqar, which had taken place in
853 BCE. Thus the stela probably dates from 853–852 BCE (Younger 2000: 261).
[23]Lemaire 1998: 9. The Dan Stela, generally known as the Tel Dan Stela, is an inscription in Aramaic
written on basalt that was retrieved in a secondary context (though during controlled excavations)
at the site of Tel Dan in northern Israel. It was found in three pieces (one in 1993 and two in 1994).
After much scholarly debate, it is now generally agreed that the inscription is authentic and that most
probably it was set up by Hazael of Aram-Damascus. Most scholars now also agree that the Tel Dan
Stela dates from the ninth century BCE and that it refers to the Davidic dynasty when it employs the
phrase "house of David".
[24]Lemaire 1998: 10.
[25]Lemaire 1998: 10.

to the event narrated (in this case the Kurkh Monolith) is more reliable than the later inscription of Shalmaneser III, who seems to be boasting rather than narrating a true historical event.[26] In the light of all this, one can view the Tel Dan inscription as a monument that was set up for propaganda purposes, which, however, also contains precise information, such as that Ahab had two thousand chariots.[27] Indeed, this monument can be viewed as "a small piece of Aramaic royal historiography which contains important historical informations [*sic*] and interpretations about the kingdoms of Damascus, Israel and Judah in the second half of the ninth century".[28]

The exilic period proves to be one about which we had scant information about the Judaean community in exile in Babylon. It is true that Ezekiel was one of the biblical writers who in part had already shown us that the exiles were settled together "rather than [being] completely dispersed among the new host population".[29] However, in and of itself the biblical information is sparse and we do not really have any significant details about the Judaeans in exile. Archaeology has now filled in many of the gaps by providing us with very important inscribed artefacts, such as the inscriptions in Akkadian from āl-Yaḫūdu and Našar. While these texts are largely economic, they do "include many personal names, some eighty of which are Yahwistic (about 15 percent of the total number). This helps explain how the Judeans could maintain social cohesion and develop new forms of leadership."[30] Indeed, we can now see more clearly how the Judaean community in exile in Babylon could develop new forms of leadership, such as the renewed importance of the

---

[26]Lemaire 1998: 11.

[27]The Tel Dan Stela puts to rest the debate that had surrounded the reliability or otherwise regarding the figure of the 2,000 chariots of Ahab mentioned in the Kurkh Monolith. There had been scholars on both sides: those who viewed this figure as the result of a scribal error and others who saw it as correct (Younger 2000: 263). The Tel Dan Stela supports the view of the latter group.

[28]Lemaire 1998: 11.

[29]Williamson 2015: 13.

[30]Williamson 2015: 13.

heads of the extended family, namely the elders, and the increased authority of the priests.[31]

Scholars have classified the Akkadian documents that refer to the Judaeans in exile in Babylon into three archival groups: on the basis of geographical information, names, and individuals' activities and their "familial and social interlocutors".[32] The first group of documents comes from Āl-Yahūdu and is consequently known as the Judah town group. The second group focuses on the town of Našar and can be split into two subgroups: (a) that which has yielded a few Hebrew and Yahwistic names; (b) that which contains plenty of West Semitic names. Finally, the third group of texts focuses on the town of Bīt-Abī-râm and on the royal official Zababa-šar-uṣur. This is the best that can be done given that we lack a good archaeological context "for almost all Neo-Babylonian records".[33] We do know, however, that those texts exhibiting links with each other at roughly the same time most probably stemmed from the same archaeological contexts. The three groups of texts just mentioned "most likely survived the last millennia in close proximity to each other, where they were finally disposed of or set aside by their ancient owners, presumably in an urban administrative center in the region".[34]

The foregoing points show that we have enough to go on in order to gain interesting information regarding the Judaean community in exile in Babylon. The Āl-Yahūdu archive and the archives of neighbouring towns span the Neo-Babylonian and Achaemenid periods, specifically from 572 BCE till 477 BCE. The tablets are all written in Babylonian with the exception of a few short glosses in Aramaic script in the margins,[35] and the earliest tablet is dated to the twentieth day of Nisannu in the thirty-third year of Nebuchadnezzar

[31]Williamson 2015: 13.
[32]Pearce and Wunsch 2014: 7.
[33]Pearce and Wunsch 2014: 9.
[34]Pearce and Wunsch 2014: 9.
[35]Gross 2016.

II's reign, namely 572 BCE.[36] The place that is mentioned most frequently in the Āl-Yaḫūdu archive is Ālu-ša-Našar (the town of Našar) or Bīt-Našar ([town of] Našar's house). Another place name worthy of note is Āl-Yaḫūdu (Judah town), which in two early texts appears as Āl-Yaḫūdāya—that is to say, the town of the Judaeans. The names of some individuals surface both in Āl-Yaḫūdu and in Bīt-Našar.[37]

The aforementioned Babylonian texts provide a link with certain biblical information besides giving us new insights into the Judaean community in exile. Thus, there is a link with Ezek. 1:1, where we find mention of the river Chebar. In the light of Isa. 10:21 it is possible that the name Yašubu-Ṣidiqu in the Babylonian records is an indirect reference to the exile, whilst it is very interesting to note that in 2 Chron. 25:28 Jerusalem is called "the city of Judah", which is echoed in the place name Āl-Yaḫūdu (Judah town) mentioned above. This means that this place turns out to be the Jerusalem of Babylon and this fits perfectly with the chronology of the Āl-Yaḫūdu tablets dating to between 587 BCE and 450 BCE, thus filling the gap between the exile and 450 BCE.[38]

The Āl-Yaḫūdu tablets throw a great deal of light on 2 Chron. 25:28 not only by providing further incontrovertible archaeological evidence that "the city of Judah" was an alternative name for Jerusalem, but also by coming to the aid of those scholars who deal with the textual criticism of this verse. The context of this verse is the death of Amaziah and it tells us that he was buried in "the city of Judah", which clearly refers to Jerusalem. Some manuscripts of 2 Chron. 25:28 together with the parallel text of 2 Kgs 14:20 read "the city of David" instead of "the city of Judah". Which is the likely original reading? Although Edward Lewis Curtis and Albert Alonzo Madsen are aware of the fact that "in the Assyrian inscriptions Asarhaddon called Manasseh king of *the city of Judah*" still they decide to view "the city of Judah" as being "clearly

---

[36]Pearce and Wunsch 2014: 4.
[37]Pearce and Wunsch 2014: 6.
[38]Gross 2016.

a scribal error" and they therefore opt for "the city of David" as the likely original reading.[39] However, it is clear that "the city of Judah" is here the *lectio difficilior* and that on *a priori* grounds it should be preferred to "the city of David".

In view of this it is better to go along with Raymond B. Dillard who, besides making a reference to "city of Judah" as an alternative name for Jerusalem in extra-biblical sources, also reminds us that in fact the Chronicler would have referred to Jerusalem as the city of Judah (just as was the common practice in extra-biblical sources), but which he labels as "city of David" in various places simply by way of creating a harmonization with this latter ordinary and more common biblical designation of Jerusalem. Indeed, "it is far easier to account for the correction ['city of Judah' into 'city of David'] than to explain a change to 'Judah'; therefore, MT[40] is likely original in this case in spite of the preponderance of external evidence".[41] This also tallies perfectly well with "the practice of referring to a city by the name of a kingdom or a nation that inhabited it".[42] Thus we find "city of Moab" (Isa. 15:1), "city of Amalek" (1 Sam. 15:5), and "city of Judah" (2 Chron. 25:28).[43] This latter designation in 2 Chron. 25:28 is a *hapax* in the Hebrew Bible, but in view of the foregoing observations it is clear that it can be endorsed as the better reading especially when we keep in mind the fact that Akkadian sources refer to Jerusalem as "the city of Judah" in more than one instance; indeed, this was often the practice from the time of the Judaean monarchy onwards.[44]

---

[39] Lewis and Madsen 1910: 447.

[40] "MT" stands for Masoretic text, which is the text of the Hebrew Bible that Jewish scholars, called Masoretes, established, and which consists of consonants, vowel signs, accents (which could also function as punctuation marks and musical signs for chanting the biblical text), as well as notes. The oldest *complete* Masoretic manuscript of the Hebrew Bible is the Leningrad Codex (c. 1009 CE).

[41] Dillard 1987: 197.

[42] Kalimi 2005: 65.

[43] Kalimi 2005: 65. From the period of the Judaean monarchy onwards, one possible way of referring to the city of Jerusalem in Akkadian literature was by labelling it as "the city of Judah" (Kalimi 2005: 100–1).

[44] See the previous note.

The Āl-Yahūdu tablets also show us that the Judaeans in Babylon were experiencing a certain amount of acculturation in view of the fact that their personal names include Yahwistic elements that were joined to Neo-Babylonian name features.[45] Thus, for example, the name of the individual Yahu-šar-uṣur (Yahu protect the king) also appears as Bēl-šar-uṣur (Bēl, protect the king).[46] This is highly interesting, especially in view of the fact that this person appears in "three promissory notes", all of which date from Nebuchadnezzar's reign to that of Nabonidus, thus clearly indicating that *early* in the exilic period "an individual Judean could already achieve degrees of financial and social prosperity".[47] The evidence shows that the Judaeans in exile in Babylon had even integrated themselves in the "administrative structures" of their place of exile.[48]

Notwithstanding all this, it seems that the Judaean exiles kept together as a close-knit community. The Babylonian archives mentioned above reveal that Amurru is found as a theophoric element, clearly indicating that some people worshipped this deity. Thus, for example, we find the personal name Amurru-šar-uṣur (Amurru protect the king). There are fifteen Amurru names traceable to nineteen individuals, showing us that these persons formed part of the West Semites living near the exiles from Judah. However, although the following is an argument from silence, still it is of interest to learn that "no individual bearing an Amurru name is yet attested among the heavily Judean population of Āl-Yahūdu".[49]

[45]Pearce and Wunsch 2014: 28–9.
[46]Pearce and Wunsch 2014: 46, 90. Bēl is actually a title meaning "Lord", and it could refer to various gods "as head of their local pantheon". Thus, for example, in Babylon it refers to Marduk (Dalley 2000: 318). One should note that the Yahwistic element in the Judaean personal names that we find in the Babylonian archives mentioned above appears either as *yāhû* ("almost exclusively in the initial position") or as *yāma* (in the final position); see Pearce and Wunsch 2014: 19. The "m" in *yāma* can be accounted for in view of the fact that Hebrew "waw" is rendered by Babylonian "m". Indeed, it is common in Babylonian to transcribe the "w" of foreign names with an "m" (Eissfeldt 1963: 90).
[47]Pearce and Wunsch 2014: 29.
[48]Pearce and Wunsch 2014: 29.
[49]Pearce and Wunsch 2014: 13.

The above-mentioned variants—Āl-Ya<u>h</u>ūdu and Alu-ša-Yahūdāya—used to refer to Judah in the Babylonian texts are highly interesting. The former name shows us that the Babylonians were aware of the "village of Judaea", whilst the latter shows that they also made reference to the "village of the Judaeans"—thus leaving no doubt that the majority of the Judaean exiles in these places came from Judaea and "probably even from Jerusalem itself, since Yahūd(u) was used in antiquity as a designation both for the province of Judea and for its capital, Jerusalem".[50] This fits squarely with the biblical data that show that it was the elite amongst the Judaeans who were taken into exile in Babylon.

The study of both inscribed and uninscribed artefacts (whether found in archaeological investigations or not) proves to be very fruitful even for the biblical texts of the New Testament. One important case is that of the word "politarch". This term is "a Macedonian title for non-Roman magistrates".[51] It is interesting that "excavations in Northern Greece have produced approximately seventy inscriptions that mention politarchs".[52] In Macedonia the Greek title "politarch" stood for "magistrates of free Greek cities" as opposed to "Roman magistrates with Roman titles".[53] Each city had to have a minimum of one politarch and a maximum of seven (or more, depending on its size). The task of the politarch was to enforce the law where civic issues were concerned.[54] We encounter this word only twice in the Bible, namely in Acts 17:6 and 8, where it turns out to be the title that was given to the officials of the city of Thessalonica, a sea port and capital of the province of Macedonia. In this context we see that the politarchs restored calm in the city after the uproar in Jason's house, and in the light of the aforementioned information

[50]Abraham 2011: 264.
[51]Matthews 2018: 1988.
[52]Devries 2009: 559.
[53]Devries 2009: 559.
[54]Devries 2009: 559.

that archaeology has yielded we can understand why it was precisely the politarchs who restored order. The inscriptional evidence about the politarchs shows that Luke was using the precise Greek term for the officials in charge at Thessalonica during the first century CE. Inscriptional evidence regarding the politarchate comes from Macedonia, Thessaly, Illyria, Bithynia, Egypt, and the Greek islands, but the bulk comes from Macedonia, and from within this province the majority of the inscriptions were found in Thessalonica.[55]

The points discussed in this chapter go to show how important it is to use every piece of evidence in order to study past human societies. It also calls for us to remember that much of our evidence comes from archaeology. All artefacts (*inscribed and uninscribed*, whether found in archaeological excavations or not) have to be studied carefully and the respective results brought to bear on each other in a methodologically appropriate manner, which in essence means after each datum has been analyzed according to the canons proper to the discipline to which it belongs.[56] Along the way scholars might discover that the results of archaeology could very well match and enhance in a very smooth manner those of biblical scholarship, such as is the case with the Āl-Yaḫūdu tablets discussed above, which throw important light on the Judaean community in exile. On the other hand, there are instances where the integration of the results of archaeological and biblical research is not that straightforward, though, nevertheless, it can still make a very good contribution to the history of ancient Israel such as is the case with the period of the emergence of Israel in Canaan.[57] The crucial point is to ensure that the artefacts studied were retrieved from secure and correctly recorded findspots. Indeed, having trustworthy findspot data is the only way to guarantee that any reconstructions of the occupational history of sites and the resulting knowledge we gain about past human societies are based

---

[55]Horsley 1992: 138–9.
[56]De Vaux 1970: 70; Frendo 2011: 27–8, 105.
[57]I have dealt with this problem elsewhere; see Frendo 2004.

on solid foundations. In simple archaeological terms this means that stratigraphic excavations constitute the best guarantee that our conclusions are based on solid foundations.[58]

---

[58]When we lack this ideal scenario, at times there can be compensating factors that allow us to draw reasonably solid conclusions on the basis of the information found on certain artefacts. Such is the case with the Āl-Yaḫūdu tablets themselves, for which, unfortunately, we lack an archaeological context, but about which we can still conclude that "the appearance of whole groups of loosely related material at roughly the same time indicates that these texts most likely originate from the same locus" (Pearce and Wunsch 2014: 9).

4

Earlier, concurrent, or later? Stratigraphy as the backbone of archaeology

Archaeologists often retrieve innumerable artefacts dating from the past as they dig through different layers of earth and rubble. Often, these slices of history are full of clues that testify to past human activity. Archaeologists are fundamentally interested in understanding the occupational history of the sites they investigate, their goal being to better appreciate the cultural history of the ancient peoples who had once lived on those sites. However, it is clear that they cannot achieve these aims without gleaning from the data a clear and solid chronological sequence of events. It is important to know which artefacts were in use at any given period of time and most importantly it is crucial to understand the cultural development of all those who had once inhabited the sites in question.

There was a time when archaeologists were somewhat obsessed with chronology, specifically with ceramic chronology, often at the expense of taking other important matters into serious consideration. However, if we think very carefully about the bigger picture, it becomes clear that we definitely still need to take chronological matters into account—indeed, chronology is of the essence when it comes to tracing the development of cultures, especially when one is dealing with the developments that took place at a given site. Only in this manner can archaeologists detect whether they are dealing with a continuity of culture, or with a discontinuity—and if an answer either way can be reached, to what extent. Moreover, it is chronological considerations that can clarify such matters as trade links. If studied alongside other aspects of past human societies, chronology could be viewed as *the* foundation on which most of the statements made by archaeologists about past human societies can be constructed.[1]

The problem is that when it comes to dating ancient artefacts and the layers in which they were found it is not that easy—to say the least—to determine the correct date of the various excavated layers. The discipline of archaeology has made tremendous advances in scientific dating. So, for example, radiocarbon dating is now more secure than it ever previously was. Having said this, however, the method still has its weakness and is not absolutely precise.[2] Unfortunately, we still do not have a shockproof method of dating that can be applied to all periods of history. In archaeological terms this means that we

---

[1]Indeed, "time is one of the key elements in most attempts to define archaeology's disciplinary distinctiveness. Other people may study human societies, but along with the unique emphasis on material culture it is 'time-depth' that makes archaeological perspectives singular and, arguably, capable of contributing something to debates in other social sciences… Time is an all-pervading theme in what archaeologists do, insofar as chronology and dating underpin comparative and interpretative statements about contemporaneity or sequence, and thus change and continuity. This temporal preoccupation also informs popular discourses of archaeology as 'time-travel', or of archaeologists as 'time detectives'" (Gardner 2001: 35 and references there).

[2]As Wright (2017: 303) remarked, "Accelerator mass spectrometry has made radiocarbon dating the most precise method to determine the death of living organisms that occurred within the last 50,000 years. However, the method is not without limitations and this review article provides Africanist archaeologists with cautionary insights as to when, where, and how to utilize radiocarbon dates." As will be shown further on in this chapter, this statement is equally applicable to those archaeologists grappling with the chronological problems that beset the discussion on the existence or otherwise of a united kingdom in ancient Israel.

do not have a really secure system of what is known as absolute, or better still, chronometric dating.[3]

Notwithstanding the foregoing comments, archaeology can still help us to reconstruct the sequence of events pertaining to past human societies and their cultures by providing us with relative dating. This is a system of dating that is very reliable in that it gives us secure information as to what was anterior to what, what was concurrent with what, and what followed what on archaeological sites. Such dates are not real dates but rather sequences of events, which are reliable on condition that the excavation in question had been conducted according to the principles of archaeological stratigraphy. This means that the layers of soil have to be peeled away in the reverse order to that in which they were laid down, keeping each layer separate from the other on the basis of its colour and texture. The principle is that such an excavation will provide a solid sequence of events, allowing us to know which layer preceded which, which layers were contemporary, and which ones followed those that preceded them. The artefacts found in the various layers can thus be assigned to a given relative time that can be translated into real dates via any datable artefacts (such as coins or inscriptions that carry a date on them) in the layers, or via what is known as cross-dating.[4] In this manner the relative time sequence can be translated into real dates. The study of pottery[5] plays an important role in all this. Archaeologists create ceramic types largely on the basis of the type of clay used, the manufacturing technology employed, the shape of the pottery vessels, and, where applicable, decoration. They then compare the pottery types found on different sites with each other, going on to

---

[3]This is a "dating method that provides an actual age in years for a defined piece of material or event. Because all such dates are, in statistical terms, estimates, the results are usually reported with a measure of probability, typically expressed as a standard deviation" (Darvill 2002: 85–6).

[4]In this dating method "stratigraphic or assemblage similarities between sites within a region can be used (much in the same way that tree rings are matched) to extend known dates from one or more sites to sites where chronometric techniques might not work, allowing archaeologists to develop cohesive chronologies for exploring regional social and cultural evolution over time" (Michaels 1996: 169).

[5]For an excellent textbook on pottery studies in archaeology, see Orton and Hughes 2013.

date the pottery and the layers on various sites on the basis of similar pottery types that appear on comparable sites with layers whose dates are known. It is clear, however, that when ceramic dating is used in cross-dating (as is often the case in the archaeology of the southern Levant) things can get fuzzy, since pottery of a certain date on one site can continue to be used at a *later stage* on a different site.

Moreover, there is another snag in that all current methods of the scientific dating of pottery are either not wholly reliable, or are still in their infancy.[6] This means that in large part the dating of ceramic finds is ultimately based on the type of cross-dating mentioned above. This is why we have to be extremely cautious when it comes to appealing to pottery dates in order to either buttress or demolish dates linked to important historical events.

I would like to illustrate the points discussed thus far via a case study in Biblical Archaeology, namely to examine whether the results of archaeological research necessarily lead us to abandon a tenth-century BCE date for the archaeological artefacts (and the associated material, such as architectural remains) traditionally attributed to the Solomonic period, dating them instead to the ninth-century BCE. This question emerged when the excavations at Tel Jezreel revealed a very large enclosure that had been destroyed, and that was deemed to have been linked with the information found in 1 Kings regarding the enclosure of Ahab and Jezebel. Archaeologists attributed the destruction to the late ninth century BCE, concluding that it was probably Hazael of Damascus who had destroyed the enclosure shortly after the end of the Omride dynasty c. 840/830 BCE. The next step was to conclude that the pottery that stemmed from the destroyed enclosure had to be dated to the ninth century BCE. However, it transpired that the same type of pottery was also found in nearby Megiddo in buildings that traditionally had been linked with King Solomon and which had therefore been dated to the tenth century

---

[6]Orton and Hughes 2013: 224–5.

BCE. In view of this, Israel Finkelstein lowered the dates of the Megiddo buildings to the ninth century BCE.[7] Even if we assume that it is very likely that the destruction of the enclosure at Tel Jezreel can be linked with Hazael and that it can therefore be dated to the ninth century BCE, in no way does it follow that the same type of pottery at Megiddo must be dated to the ninth century BCE since it is possible that this type of pottery was in use there in the tenth century BCE and was still being used at Tel Jezreel in the following century.[8] Be that as it may, the most important point to note is that in fact similar pottery was found at Tel Jezreel itself in in-fill layers of buildings situated *under* the foundations of the enclosure and therefore linked to an earlier town or village before the enclosure was built. The corollary of all this is that at Tel Jezreel itself the ninth-century pottery linked to the destruction of the enclosure was already in use in the pre-Omride period, namely the tenth or early ninth century BCE. The evidence simply shows that the same type of pottery was used in much of the tenth *and* the ninth century BCE. This goes to show that only a careful analysis of the stratigraphic evidence and a critical use of cross-dating allow us to draw reasonable conclusions whereby the results of archaeological research can be linked to any relevant historical information present in the biblical texts.

The points raised in the foregoing paragraph would need a much more extensive and thorough treatment if justice were to be done to the complex nature of the issue in question. However, I would like to restrict myself to simply pinning down the type of reasoning that a biblical scholar should exercise when bringing in archaeological evidence to either buttress or deny the historicity of certain events mentioned in the biblical text. In this context it is interesting to be aware of what the starting point for the lowering of

---

[7]Mazar 2007c: 119.

[8]As Williamson (2015: 10) too pointed out, pottery found in different layers does not necessarily date to the same time, since as he very aptly put it "the pottery may be early at Megiddo and simply still in use at later Jezreel".

the Iron Age chronology[9] of Israel was. In actual fact, as Benjamin Mazar points out, it all started with David Ussishkin, who had lowered "the initial Philistine settlement by about 50 years", thereby causing a "snowball effect" on the chronology of the Iron Age I of Israel.[10] However, one should note that this proposal has not been accepted by those who work in Philistia and by Aegean ceramic specialists who stick to dating the first Philistine settlement in the first half of the twelfth century BCE. Finkelstein based himself on the starting point just mentioned and consequently began dating the end of the Iron Age I not to c. 1000 BCE but to c. 920/900 BCE. The result was that a host of destructions (such as Megiddo VIA and Tell Qasile X)[11] that had traditionally been dated to c. 1000 BCE were now being linked to Sheshonq I's raid of c. 920 BCE.[12] The historical implications were immense, since these results—if correct—meant that the cause of the destructions just mentioned was neither an earthquake (for Megiddo VIA and in the case of Tell Qasile X) nor King David, but Sheshonq.[13] However, radiocarbon dates for these same sites confirm the traditional date of c. 1000 BCE "or slightly later".[14]

---

[9]Scholars label the period c. 1200–586 BCE as the Iron Age. They generally subdivide this period as follows: Iron Age I (= IAI): c. 1200–1025 BCE; Iron Age II (= IAII): c. 1025–586 BCE, which in turn can be subdivided into Iron Age IIA (c. 1025–928 BCE); Iron Age IIB (= IAIIB) (c. 928–722 BCE); and Iron Age IIC (= IAIIC) (c. 722–586 BCE). This is the periodization of the Iron Age that *The New Oxford Annotated Bible* employs (Coogan 2018: 2308–10).

[10]Mazar 2014: 355 and references there.

[11]A number of archaeologists use numerals (generally Roman) to denote an archaeological period on a site. Unfortunately, this could be confusing to the novice. Strictly speaking, *stratum* is the Latin word for layer, and therefore per se it should stand for the smallest indivisible unit of stratigraphy, such as a layer of soil. Layers are grouped into phases that show significant changes (such as architectural ones) in the various areas of a site, whilst phases can be grouped into periods which indicate changes that took place over a whole site—such as major architectural ones, or destructions. Although an archaeological period could overlap with an historical one, it is important to note that this is not necessarily so, and that the two are not identical (see also, n. 34 below). Thus, various archaeological periods on a site could span simply one historical period—such as, for example, the Hellenistic period (333–63 BCE). Archaeologists of the southern Levant are amongst those who use the word stratum to signify an archaeological period, and hence the many such references in this chapter and elsewhere in this monograph.

[12]Mazar 2014: 356.

[13]Mazar 2009: 329–30.

[14]Mazar 2014: 356.

If we accept the low chronology as just outlined, then the architectural remains at the sites that were traditionally attributed to Solomon would now have Ahab as their author. Indeed, as Mazar has pointed out, "in each of Finkelstein's papers on this issue, the archaeological discussion is inter-mingled with an evaluation of state formation in Israel and Judah in a manner that does not allow for any differentiation between cause and effect".[15] To make matters even worse, the results of radiocarbon dating are not always that clear cut and therefore it is important in this context to keep sight of the overall pattern and not just to appeal to one or two cases. In a certain sense the results provided by radiocarbon dating flew in the face of Finkelstein's aforementioned conclusion, and yet he persisted in making the Iron Age I in some peripheral areas last until the time of Sheshonq I and in this he was proven right. How come? Things are so because of what I mentioned in the previous paragraph, namely that pottery types which can be dated to the ninth century BCE could very well simply be testifying to a continuity of a ceramic culture that was largely the hallmark of the tenth century BCE. The evidence seems to point in this direction and a few examples will hopefully clarify the basic issues.

There is evidence for a number of Iron Age IIA contexts that cannot be later than the tenth century BCE, and this of itself contradicts Finkelstein's aim at re-dating *all* the tenth-century BCE pottery to the ninth century BCE. So, for example, radiocarbon dates from Khirbet Qeiyafa place the transition between the Iron Age I and the beginning of Iron Age IIA to the late eleventh century BCE/first half of the tenth century BCE. The same holds for Stratum XII at Arad, which is the earliest Iron Age settlement at the site—from this period we have an "Iron IIA assemblage" that *predates* Sheshonq I's invasion of Canaan since he mentions the settlement of Arad in the list of towns that he conquered. Similarly, we encounter the same situation at Megiddo, where

---

[15]Mazar 2007c: 119.

the Iron Age IIA of Stratum VB dates to the tenth century BCE, "preceding Sheshonq's attack" on the site.[16]

However, the situation is not that simple and it is crucial not to project what was happening at a few sites onto the whole land and to re-date to a later period all that material culture, most of which could have simply continued from an earlier date into a subsequent period. In the case of Tel Jezreel and Tel Rehov the results of radiocarbon dating show that the Iron Age IIA "continued well into the ninth century B.C.E.".[17] In view of the evidence that I referred to in the previous paragraph, and in view of the radiocarbon date just mentioned, we are bound to conclude that the Low Chronology of Finkelstein was correct with respect to some sites; in fact, this led Mazar to endorse the traditional chronology but in a somewhat revised condition and not in a wholesome manner. Thus, Mazar speaks of a "Modified Conventional Chronology", taking this to mean that the range of Iron Age IIA can be viewed as lasting longer than traditionally thought, namely from c. 980–830 BCE. This conclusion is based on the solid results from Tel Jezreel and Tel Rehov and it helps us to account more clearly for the "ambiguous" radiocarbon date results for Stratum H-5 from the renewed excavations at Megiddo. This stratum corresponds to Yadin's "Solomonic" city, namely his Stratum IVB-VA, and the radiocarbon dates for Stratum H-5 are both problematic and highly interesting in that some dates are late tenth century BCE whilst others give a reading similar to those from the ninth century BCE. This state of affairs, together with the pottery coming from within the in-fill layer below the palace at Tel Jezreel discussed above, leads us to the inevitable conclusion that at some sites the pottery traditionally dated to the tenth century BCE lasted longer than previously thought and was still in use in the ninth century BCE. We thus have a long period of use

---

[16]Mazar 2014: 356–7 and references there.
[17]Mazar 2014: 357.

for the same type of pottery and we can therefore now speak of an early Iron IIA and a late Iron IIA.[18]

The foregoing results mean that at Tel Rehov the transition from early Iron IIA to late Iron IIA would have occurred at some time during the last quarter of the tenth century BCE. Mazar thinks that, as far as Megiddo is concerned, the best suggestion is that of Ussishkin, namely to link the city with the two palaces (= Stratum IVA-VB) to both the tenth and the ninth centuries BCE in the sense that the city would have been founded in the tenth century during the Solomonic era, with occupancy continuing into the ninth century. Hence the above-mentioned list of Sheshonq I that mentioned Megiddo, as well as the fragments of this Pharaoh's monumental stela at the site. Indeed, "it is inconceivable that Sheshonq referred to the poor town of Stratum VB which preceded IV-VA".[19]

The points discussed thus far do not allow us to solve in a definitive manner the problem of whether the monumental structures at Megiddo, Hazor, and Gezer are necessarily linked to Solomon. At present, archaeological research cannot prove that this is so, but neither does it prove that they cannot be linked to Solomon. The issue is still an open question. However, the archaeological points raised thus far do allow us to conclude that it is still *possible* to propose a tenth-century BCE date to this monumental architecture. In fact, 1 Kgs 9:15-19 "can still be taken as a source relating to the tenth century B.C.E.".[20] It is important to read this passage closely and therefore to take note of its immediate context. Verses 15-19 form part of vv. 15-23, which overall deal with Solomon's state building projects that were carried out not by Israelites, but by forced labourers from amongst the descendants of those people whom the Israelites had not completely destroyed. The author of vv. 15-23 wants to underscore the fact that Solomon carried out his building

---

[18]Mazar 2014: 358.
[19]Mazar 2014: 358.
[20]Mazar 2014: 358.

projects through corvée labour (see especially vv. 21-22).[21] Actually, it is v. 15a that introduces the theme of forced labour that is presented in vv. 20-23, with vv. 15b-19 forming an insertion that consists of the list of Solomon's building or rebuilding activities.[22] In these verses, the information that Pharaoh had destroyed Gezer and its Canaanite inhabitants and then handed it as dowry to his daughter (Solomon's wife) functions as a parenthesis. The list in vv. 15b-19 is "of original archival type"[23] and it informs us about Solomon's activities, inter alia in Jerusalem, Hazor, Megiddo, and Gezer.

It is important to keep the points discussed thus far in view also when discussing whether David and Solomon presided over a Jerusalem that was a substantial entity to be reckoned with or whether it was simply a small backwater place. Mazar reminds us of the "massive structures" around the Gihon spring dating to the Middle Bronze Age but which continued to be used in the Iron Age; in fact, a few Iron Age walls abut the strongholds in question. The remains of the large structures just mentioned can help us to account for the important role that Jerusalem played in the Amarna letters and to better appreciate its special "status" in the story of the hill country.[24]

For biblical scholars, it is important to know whether archaeology can help to decide whether there ever was or not a United Monarchy under David and Solomon. On the available evidence, archaeology cannot answer this question directly. However, even the fact just mentioned in the foregoing paragraph together with other considerations point in the direction that we can speak of a "strong" state of Israel in the tenth century BCE which later emerged as a more developed entity in the ninth century. If we were to "deconstruct" the United Monarchy of the tenth century BCE, then we would have to grapple with the problem of how to account for "the rapid emergence in the 9th

---

[21]Wiseman (1993: 277), for example, tags 1 Kgs 9:15-23 with the words "The use of forced labour".
[22]Montgomery 1951: 205.
[23]Montgomery 1951: 205.
[24]Mazar 2014: 359.

century of fully mature royal architecture and a new material culture within a short time-span of less than 50 years".[25] I think that this latter position caters well for "a gradual development" of statehood in Israel during the tenth and ninth centuries BCE.[26]

This scenario of a royal statehood in the tenth century BCE (albeit on a smaller scale than that depicted in the biblical texts) is buttressed by various archaeological data. As already mentioned above, the ninth-century BCE pottery found at Tel Jezreel was also retrieved in the pre-Omride construction fills excavated there. Hence the pottery in question dates to the tenth *and* ninth centuries, as already discussed above. Comparative relative chronology seems to support the traditional tenth-century BCE date for the pottery in question, clearly without denying that this could have continued into the ninth century BCE, as in the case of Tel Jezreel. Arad is mentioned in Sheshonq I's list and therefore the earliest settlement there must date to the tenth century BCE, namely to Solomon's time. Mazar reminds us that the earliest stratum at Arad in the excavations of Yohanan Aharoni was Stratum XII. The pottery from this stratum is similar to pottery found in Judah that was traditionally dated to the tenth century BCE and the same pattern obtains at Lachish and Beersheba. As pointed out above, according to Finkelstein's low chronology all this pottery should be dated to the ninth century BCE, but surprisingly enough he "himself accepts the dating of Arad Stratum XII to the time period *prior* to Sheshonq, and by doing so he pulls the rug from underneath his own theory".[27] For the sake of fairness one should add that it is true that Kathleen Kenyon had dated pottery groups from Samaria to the ninth century BCE, but a re-examination of this pottery now shows that Samaria was also occupied in Iron Age I.[28] Hence, the ceramic evidence itself supports the scenario already

[25]Mazar 2003: 94 and references there.
[26]Mazar 2003: 94.
[27]Mazar 2007c: 121 (my italics).
[28]Knoppers 1997: 28–9 and references there.

discussed above that the "tenth-century pottery" continued to be used in the ninth century, with the result that we cannot simply divorce the monumental architecture mentioned above from the tenth century BCE, and hence from the period of the United Monarchy.

Notwithstanding all the aforementioned points, one should reiterate that in the last analysis pottery chronology can be both imprecise and deceptive, as the discussion above shows. So, we turn to radiocarbon dating in the hope that we can achieve absolute dates, or more precisely chronometric dates.

When radiocarbon dating is used in an attempt to decide whether we should opt for the traditional Iron Age I chronology or prefer Finkelstein's Low Chronology we find a highly confusing impasse. On its own, radiocarbon dating cannot solve the problem since the results are not consistent; indeed, at times they are virtually contradictory. Thus, the early results seemed to be in support of Finkelstein's position, namely that we should opt for c. 900 BCE as the date marking the end of Iron Age I. However, when these results were checked again they gave a date lying between 964 and 944 BCE to mark the transition from Iron Age I to Iron Age II. Consequently it becomes apparent that radiocarbon dating has got its problems, since "new published dates or elimination of published dates for certain reasons (such as outliers, wood samples that are much too old, and questionable contexts or dates), may change the results substantially".[29]

By now it should have become clear that both ceramic chronology and radiocarbon dating have intrinsic problems which preclude them from giving us clear-cut results that could allow us to haul them in to help us decide whether they support or otherwise a tenth-century BCE Monarchy in Israel that was a substantial social entity. However, if we include stratigraphy in the equation, then we stand a chance of getting some solid results. In point of fact, the excavations at Tel Reḥov do give us a way out of the

---

[29]Mazar 2007c: 123 and references there.

impasse. *Three separate layers*, ranging in date from the tenth to the ninth century BCE and thus spanning the time of the United Monarchy as well as the Omride dynasty, were found. All three layers had the same type of pottery groups and both historical periods in question are "to be included in a more lengthy, single archaeological period. Therefore, it would be very difficult to date with any great precision a specific structure or artefact found in this period [archaeological, stratigraphic] to either of these centuries".[30] In simple terms, this means that Mazar's above-mentioned Modified Conventional Chronology is correct and that it allows us to view the Iron Age IIA as dating from c. 980 to 840/830 BCE[31] thus spanning the tenth and most of the ninth centuries BCE. Hence, archaeological stratigraphy, pottery analysis, and radiocarbon dating allow us to conclude that various archaeological layers having the same type of pottery span the tenth and the ninth centuries BCE and that there is no question at all of an either/or situation. The same pottery is found in layers pertaining to both centuries; thus, for example, we also find that "the pottery from the Strata X-VIII at Arad is almost identical, illustrating the longevity in the pottery production in Judah".[32]

Indeed, the points discussed thus far show that archaeology does not allow us to say that it has produced evidence that would negate that there ever was a United Monarchy. In this context, it is very important to note two essentially simple but very important points. The first is to keep in mind the fact that an archaeological period is not necessarily equivalent to a historical period. From the purely archaeological point of view, a period is a term of stratigraphy that indicates any major activity (such as an architectural one) that is evidenced across the whole of a site.[33] This means that there could be two different

---

[30]Schmidt 2007: 103–4.

[31]Mazar 2007: 121.

[32]Mazar 2007b: 165.

[33]Indeed, an activity "being 'site wide' defines a 'period'" (Roskams 2001: 260), and that is why "the sequence of the phases can be grouped into *large* amalgamations called 'periods'" (Harris 1989: 115 [my italics]). I thank Professor Nicholas C. Vella who kindly informed me about Roskams' book.

historical periods that belong to one archaeological period, as is the case with Tel Reḥov mentioned in the foregoing paragraph. The second important point to note is that radiocarbon dating (as already shown) can produce different dates for the same sample and that it is not always that secure. We do well to use it, but we should also keep in mind the fact that absolute dates, including those resulting from the use of radiocarbon dating, "achieve their authoritative status as scientific fact by ignoring other times. The intrinsic times of material culture being used are subordinated—relegated in favour of a series of 'terminal times'; this so-called 'absolute time' is nothing less than the time of organic decay—it is in fact statistical, probabilistic time with all its attendant uncertainties".[34]

It is thus clear that we cannot use archaeology to demonstrate that there never was a United Monarchy. The issues of dating discussed thus far make it clear that we do not have to necessarily date to the Omride period of the ninth century BCE the monumental architecture that had traditionally been dated to the tenth century. In truth, what we now have is a low chronology and an "amended high" one; the proponents of both camps argue that Iron Age IIB begins toward the end of the ninth century BCE, but they disagree as to when Iron Age IIA begins. One group chooses the end of the tenth century BCE, whilst the other (and this includes Mazar) opts for the first half of this century. Thus it is interesting to note that when it comes to relating the results of archaeology with those of biblical research, we find that we "can still support the biblical chronology of *at least* the end of Solomon's kingdom within Iron IIA", but the low chronology "does not" allow us to do so.[35]

The main problem is that the available data do not allow us to make any definitive conclusions. It goes without saying that we have to be very precise and cautious when it comes to correlating the results of archaeology with those of biblical scholarship, always wary of not falling into the trap of

[34]McGlade 1999: 142–3.
[35]Sharon 2014: 60 (my italics).

generalizations or of not considering multiple facets of any given problem. Mazar himself has shown that the results are not always clear. Thus, when it comes to interpreting the data from Megiddo, we are faced with two possible scenarios. The traditional picture is that Stratum IVB-VA (the Palaces City) was dated to the tenth century BCE and attributed to Solomon, whilst Stratum IVA (the "Stables City") was dated to the ninth century BCE and attributed to Ahab. Finkelstein's strong belief in his proposed Low Chronology led to his setting up the other scenario, namely that of dating Stratum IVB-VA (the Palaces City) to the ninth century BCE and attributing it to Ahab, whilst dating Stratum IVA (the Stables City and the six-chambered gate) to the eighth century BCE and attributing it to Manasseh. In this particular case, Mazar's own Modified Conventional Chronology mentioned above "enables one to date the pottery found in the 'palaces city' to either the time of Solomon or to the time of Ahab. This situation demonstrates the variety of possibilities in the interpretation of archaeological data for historical reconstruction."[36]

In view of the points discussed thus far, it seems that Mazar's Modified Conventional Chronology is supported by the evidence of the revised radio-carbon dating results themselves, and, as already noted, these do not negate the possibility of still attributing the pottery traditionally dated to the tenth century BCE to this date. This would mean that we could still attribute to Solomon the archaeological periods traditionally linked to him, with the result that we could still say that there is no specific evidence that negates the possibility of there having been a United Monarchy in ancient Israel. This is a very thorny issue and the best solution for the moment is to leave it all as an open question from the archaeological point of view. In brief, this means that archaeology can—for the moment at least—neither confirm nor deny that there was a substantial political and social entity in ancient Israel during the time of King Solomon. In this context it is important to recall that various

---

[36]Mazar 2007c: 131.

disciplines (including history, and thus the historical information relayed in the Bible, as well as archaeology) suffer from gaps in memory that do not allow us to view the whole picture of the past.

The foregoing paragraph indicates clearly that we have to reckon with gaps in the record, whether historical, archaeological, or indeed even geological. In fact, geology has gaps in some of its own stratigraphic sequences. Volcanic eruptions and "orogenics (the deformation of the earth's crust to form mountains)" could be absent from a geological record.[37] Thus, for example, in the Grand Canyon there is a gap of c. 1,130 million years that is missing from the record, and it is true to say that "geological and archaeological sequences are as riddled with flaws as is the record of historical memory, although the mechanics of 'forgetting' are in no way the same. In short, stratigraphic memory is no more objective than historical memory."[38] The result of all this is that even the discussion itself about the crucial role of stratigraphy in archaeological research mentioned above should be used very cautiously when it comes to drawing conclusions relating to historical information contained in the Bible. Indeed, when we think hard about this whole issue, we come to realize that in reality we encounter gaps in memory in all of the following areas: our individual memory that could be fraught with errors, forgetfulness of certain events, and juxtaposition of events *inter alia*; historical memory (including the historical information contained in the Bible) that is subject to the same pattern as that pertaining to the memory of individuals; geology (see the foregoing remarks); and, as just discussed, archaeology. In view of all this and of the other points dealt with in this chapter, it is legitimate to ask whether we can really date to the ninth century BCE *all* the pottery in Israel that was traditionally dated to the tenth century BCE simply because it continued in use during the following century at a few sites, such as at Tel Jezreel. Moreover, it is clear that it would be too premature to draw historical

[37]Brandfon 1987: 24 and references there.
[38]Brandfon 1987: 25.

conclusions that there were not even a few substantial architectural remains in the tenth century BCE simply on the basis of Finkelstein's aforementioned ceramic chronological proposal.

In addition to all this, it is crucial to add that ceramic chronology is ultimately based on assumptions. The excavations at Arad provide a classic example in this regard. It has been observed that at this site Strata X-VIII are "similar to each other" and that the pottery of Stratum X and Lachish Level III are "strikingly similar".[39] Archaeologists draw conclusions on the basis of such considerations, but we have to remember that such conclusions are true if the assumptions involved are themselves true. Indeed, "on the *assumption* that ceramic parallels indicate temporal proximity, the assemblage of Stratum X [at Arad] cannot be 150 years earlier; if it were, one would expect that alongside the 8th century types, some earlier elements would be preserved, as was the case at Tel 'Eton".[40] John McGlade reminds us that we should not allow things like typology and "emphasis on similarity" to obscure the diverse data we encounter, harmonizing and reducing them "to a convincing narrative supported by chronometric dating".[41] We have to read the archaeological record in all its rich variety and not allow ourselves to be trapped into putting everything into neat boxes. In this regard I think that, as shown above, Mazar's Modified Conventional Chronology, which dates to the tenth and ninth centuries BCE the pottery previously dated to the tenth century, turns out to be sound, whilst, on the other hand, Finkelstein seems to be a victim of the "emphasis on similarity" which is then linked to chronometric dating with drastic implications for historical considerations pertaining to the tenth, ninth, and eighth centuries BCE.

In truth, Finkelstein himself is very much aware that ceramic dating could be problematic. When he criticizes William G. Dever for having dated

---

[39]Zimhoni 1985: 85, 86.
[40]Zimhoni 1985: 86 (my italics).
[41]McGlade 1999: 142.

red-slipped, slipped, and hand-burnished pottery "on commonly accepted *ceramic* grounds", Finkelstein correctly says: "but red-slipped and burnished pottery does not carry a date label".[42] If this is true, then this statement has to equally apply to Finkelstein himself when he dates to the ninth century BCE all the pottery that was traditionally assigned a tenth-century BCE date. All this shows how weak the foundations on which statements related to the history of ancient Israel can be, especially when those foundations and statements are based on ceramic chronology.

The problems become even more acute if we add architectural considerations to the equation. If we hold on to the tenth century BCE as the date for the pottery traditionally ascribed to this century, then we have to reckon with the fact that many scholars draw the logical conclusion of attributing the city gates at Hazor, Megiddo, and Gezer to King Solomon, seeing them as following the same blueprint. However, not all scholars agree on this. Thus, for example, Ussishkin has pointed out that the plan of the gate at Gezer is c. 17.0 m square, whilst the gates at Hazor and Megiddo have a rectangular plan measuring c. 17.5–18m by c. 20.3m. He adds that at Ashdod there is a six-chambered gate similar to the ones at Hazor, Megiddo, and Gezer, thus showing us that such gates were not limited to the area of ancient Israel. Indeed, Ussiskin's study tells us that six-chambered gates were popular in the tenth and the ninth centuries BCE and were thus not limited to the Solomonic period. Ussishkin has also shown that although these types of gates are all constructed in a similar manner, they are different in "size and style".[43] On the other hand, G.E. Wright argues that the gates at Hazor, Megiddo, and Gezer followed the same blueprint, except for "minor adjustments to the terrain"; in support of this claim he produced a whole range of measurements for these gates.[44] He measured the length and width of the gates, the space between the

---

[42]Finkelstein 2007: 11.
[43]Ussishkin 1980: 17.
[44]Wright 1958: 104.

towers, the width of the entrance passage, the width of the walls, as well as the width of the casemate walls adjoining the gates (in this case this datum was not found at Megiddo).[45] Yigael Yadin rebutted Ussishkin's aforementioned claim that the gates at Hazor, Megiddo, Gezer, Lachish, and Ashdod are similar. Yadin pointed out that at Gezer, Hazor, and Megiddo the six-chambered gates "are further fortified by two outer towers, built in direct continuation of the lines of the chambers", whereas at Lachish and Ashdod the towers were set at the outside of the facades resulting in the creation of a forecourt opposite the entrance.[46] Moreover, Yadin clearly states that "Ussishkin cannot evade the fact that the "Solomonic gate" at Megiddo is identical in plan and measurements with that at Hazor".[47]

Thus, archaeology shows us that neither ceramic chronology nor the architectural remains of ancient Israel in the Iron Age have provided any evidence that leads us to conclude that there was no such thing as a substantial social and political entity in Israel during Solomon's reign. On the contrary, the points discussed thus far in this chapter seem to be pointing in the opposite direction. The fact that during the tenth and ninth centuries BCE Jerusalem seems to have been isolated and that archaeology shows that its peaks of settlement had been during the eighteenth/seventeenth centuries BCE and once again during the eighth/seventh centuries BCE "with much less in between", does not, in my opinion, necessarily mean—at least in certain respects (see my comments below)—that this "effectively bars the scenario of a 10th-century empire's capital".[48] Despite its apparent strength, such reasoning smacks of an argument from silence.

In fact, there is another interesting piece of archaeological evidence (by way of inscriptions) that shows how dangerous and imprecise it is to draw

---

[45]Wright 1958: 104.
[46]Yadin 1980: 21.
[47]Yadin 1980: 22; see also Wright 1958: 104.
[48]Sass 2010: 173.

a conclusion that something did not happen or did not exist simply because no evidence for it was found in a given set of excavated data. I am referring here to inscriptions that mention King Taita, king of Palistin (Walistin), which lies in northwestern Syria/southeastern Turkey. His realm, "clearly shown by contemporary inscriptions to cover much of northwestern Syria", is deemed to have provided "the first firm evidence for a Levantine empire in the 10th century".[49] Benjamin Sass is aware that Taita's region, namely *Palistin*, is not mentioned in contemporary Assyrian records that also happen to refrain from mentioning the important contemporary site of Charchemish. Sass himself is aware that the fact that neither Palistin nor Charchemish are mentioned in contemporary Assyrian records does not mean that they did not exist. Indeed, it is a commonplace that Charchemish played an important role in the political events of the ancient Near East, and the absence of its mention in the Assyrian inscriptions of the time led Sass himself to state that "this absence [of the mention of Palistin in contemporary Assyrian records] becomes less surprising if one bears in mind that prominent Charchemish, too, is passed over in silence in the contemporary Assyrian sources".[50] If this holds good for Palistin, why should it not also hold good for Jerusalem? Admittedly the biblical texts do embellish the greatness of this capital city that Solomon ruled over, but in no way does this mean that Jerusalem was simply a backwater place during the tenth century BCE. Unfortunately Sass does not use the same yardstick for Taita and Solomon; he accepts that Taita had an empire in the tenth century BCE despite the fact that Palistin, which he ruled over, does not get any mention at all in the contemporary Assyrian records, whilst he does not accept that during the same century Solomon was ruling over a social and political entity to be reckoned with, simply because no direct evidence for this was unearthed.[51]

[49]Sass 2010: 173.
[50]Sass 2010: 173 and references there.
[51]In this regard, see two interesting articles by Alan Millard, namely Millard 1991a and 1991b.

Finkelstein and Silberman do not accept the argument that the absence of evidence for a tenth-century BCE Jerusalem during the time of David and Solomon could be explained because of erosion and later rebuilding.[52] With regard to Jerusalem during this period, they specifically write: "yet if this was a bustling royal capital with intense daily activity, at least some of its refuse would have been preserved".[53] Indeed, they go on to say that the evidence indicates that between the sixteenth century BCE and the eighth century BCE "Jerusalem shows no archaeological signs of having been a great city or the capital of a vast monarchy".[54] Yet they themselves tell us that to the south and southwest of the Temple Mount "a scatter of potsherds" from the tenth century BCE was found.[55] Could there not originally have been more than just "a scatter" of this pottery? The points discussed in the foregoing paragraph indicate that this could very well have been the case and that we have simply to stick to what the data tell us, namely that there is no extant evidence in support of such a scenario. Importantly, by employing this reasoning we are not permitted to conclude that such a scenario is proven not to have ever existed.

A contemporary example will clarify the point just mentioned. Most of us remember, and have seen many videos and photographs of, the terrifying disaster that hit New York on the 11th September 2001 when the Twin Towers were destroyed. Elsewhere I have referred to the relevant evidence that shows that out of 2,752 victims nearly 2,000 people were vaporised, the result being that there was not a shred of physical evidence that could account for them, although we know for certain that they had existed. I have also made reference elsewhere to Jennifer Wallace as one who had "reflected on the fact that there is a gap between our desire to find what we know for certain to have once

---

[52]Finkelstein and Silberman 2006: 272–4.
[53]Finkelstein and Silberman 2006: 272.
[54]Finkelstein and Silberman 2006: 274.
[55]Finkelstein and Silberman 2006: 273.

existed, and the lack of any relevant evidence stemming from archaeological excavation".[56] Indeed, in Wallace's own words "Archaeological excavation highlights this gulf all too vividly. It measures it literally, comparing the absence of evidence with the pressing compulsion to find it."[57] This is a clear illustration that the maxim "absence of evidence is not evidence of absence" is true, and it applies well to the case of Jerusalem, as already discussed in the previous paragraphs.

Some scholars try to defend the claim of those who uphold the view that Israel and Judah (and consequently Jerusalem) could not have been that important during the tenth century BCE owing to the fact that the low demographic results for these regions during this period point in the direction that there was no Israelite and Judahite state with the attendant scribal bureaucracy until the ninth and eighth centuries BCE respectively.[58] Unfortunately this argument is fraught with error since it both smacks of an argument from silence, as well as basing itself on demographic studies which when applied to ancient times are not always that reliable.[59] Indeed, "it is a fundamental methodological error to confuse impoverishment of archaeological remains with impoverishment of culture. The latter does not follow from the former."[60] In fact, Mazar has reminded us that the size of Jerusalem expanded from

---

[56]Frendo 2011: 32 and references there.

[57]Wallace 2004: 149.

[58]Knoppers 1997: 40–1.

[59]Indeed, "On the optimistic side, very rough estimates (e.g., order of magnitude) of population size are quite sufficient for most archaeological purposes… Apart from the methodological problems, the estimation of population size is difficult because data requirements are high. In the central Balkans, very small portions of late Neolithic sites have been excavated. Small-scale excavations produce small and biased samples, and any estimates based on such samples would be unreliable" (Porčić 2011: 324). The problem is a real one, especially when we realize that "the same number of houses could indicate very different population sizes, depending on the demographic scenario which actually took place" (ibid.: 329).

[60]Knoppers 1997: 41. In this regard, Knoppers (ibid.: 41 n. 128) makes reference to the late P.R.S. Moorey, who in a personal communication to him had pointed to the Kassite period in Babylon as an example of the fact that poverty of archaeological remains is not identical to poverty of culture. There could be a million and one reasons for the archaeological impoverishment, such as the accidents of discovery, erosion, looting in antiquity, and so on.

c. 4 hectares in David's time to possibly 12 hectares during Solomon's reign.[61] Moreover, at the summit of the city of Jerusalem archaeology has revealed a large citadel that was very large for the tenth century BCE indicating that it "could easily serve as a power base for a central authority".[62] More importantly, the excavations of Eilat Mazar as well as those of Kathleen Kenyon have unearthed structures in Jerusalem that have no parallel with respect to their magnitude anywhere else in Israel at the time, a detail which supports the idea of the city acting as a power base for "local rulers".[63]

More often than not it is the assumptions that scholars make, alongside their making black and white arguments, that leads them to different—indeed, at times contradictory—positions based on the same evidence! Sheshonq I's well-known invasion of Palestine in the tenth century BCE is a case in point that shows how scholars sometimes interpret general archaeological and epigraphic data in diametrically opposite ways. Knoppers saw through this problem very clearly when he most appropriately wrote: "Whereas the nonmention, and hence the noncapture, of Jerusalem in the Karnak relief is cited as verification of 1 Kgs 14:25-26 (and 2 Chron. 12:1-12) by some scholars, the same lacuna is cited by others as proof that Judah was not a state in the tenth century".[64] Knoppers does well to criticize the assumptions and black and white arguments of those he targets in the citation just made. Indeed, on what basis are we allowed to conclude that Jerusalem could not have been the centre of a state (Judah) simply because it was not mentioned as having been captured by Sheshonq I? Why not consider another possibility, one which I discussed in an earlier publication, namely "the most likely explanation for this situation is the fact that the Egyptian sources list the cities that Sheshonq actually *conquered*—which was not the case with Jerusalem. This

---

[61]Mazar 2007c: 129.
[62]Mazar 2007c: 127.
[63]Mazar 2007c: 129; see also 125, 126, 127 and references there.
[64]Knoppers 1997: 33.

explains why this city is not mentioned in the Egyptian sources. The biblical texts just cited [1 Kgs. 14: 25-26 and 2 Chr. 12: 2-9] describe Sheshonq's going up against Jerusalem with the intent of conquering it, but no actual attack or victory over the city is mentioned. Instead we are told that the pharaoh carried off the treasures of the Temple and of the royal house. This seems to be best explained as a move by Rehoboam, king of Judah at the time, to pay a heavy ransom to Sheshonq, thereby averting an actual military attack that the pharaoh had planned."[65]

Finkelstein and Silberman would not accept the foregoing proposed explanation since they believe that Sheshonq did not mention Jerusalem in his list because during his time it was simply a highland village without archaeological evidence for monumental architecture. They argue that, on the contrary, the area lying to the north of Jerusalem—which was the hub of Saul's domain—provides evidence for "a cluster of sites that were abandoned in the tenth century".[66] For Finkelstein and Silberman, what Sheshonq attacked was in fact Saul's early north Israelite territory, and lowland cities such as Megiddo, whereby he regained the "southern trade routes".[67] This viewpoint is built on the assumption that the proposed Low Chronology is correct. However, as shown above, this chronology is not tenable. Moreover, the conclusions presented by Finkelstein and Silberman do not hold also because, as already shown above, there are some archaeological remains from Jerusalem that do indicate that it could indeed have been a power base for a central authority in the tenth century BCE. Indeed, William G. Dever has rebutted the viewpoint of Finkelstein and Silberman that Judah (with Jerusalem as its capital) emerged as a true state only from the seventh century BCE onwards. He adduces archaeological evidence from various sites that goes to show that the stance of Finkelstein and Silberman is untenable. He appeals to the ninth- and

[65]Frendo 2016: 99.
[66]Finkelstein and Silberman 2006: 78.
[67]Finkelstein and Silberman 2006: 81.

eighth-century BCE levels from the following sites: Tell en-Nasbeh, Bethel, Gibeon, Beth Shemesh IIb (with evidence for a water system and a palace dating already to the tenth century BCE), En-Gedi, Tell Beit Mirsim A2, Halif VIB, Beersheba IV-III (with evidence for a well-planned city and a royal administrative centre), Arad XI-VIII, Lachish IV (with ninth-century BCE evidence for "a massively fortified regional center"[68]), and Ramat Rachel that yielded ashlar masonry dating to the eighth century BCE and which was linked to a "royal palace".[69]

Thus, it seems that during the tenth century BCE Jerusalem could have very well been the main city of the region of Judah, functioning as a socio-political entity to be reckoned with—not as grand as the biblical texts would have it, admittedly, but still quite substantial. In this regard, it is well worth citing what Mazar has to say with reference to Sheshonq's activities on the central highlands of Canaan. He reminds us that during the Late Bronze Age the Egyptians' military campaign route in Canaan was focused on the coastal plain and in the valleys in the north of the country. So why did Sheshonq cut across the hills to the north of Jerusalem? What reason could there have been for him to plan on attacking Jerusalem? Mazar very aptly writes: "What else other than the Solomonic state could have been the target? Shishak's invasion seems to have been an attempt to intervene in the situation created as a consequence of Solomon's death."[70]

Therefore, the mention of Sheshonq I's campaign in 1 Kgs 14:25-28 "cannot be explained away as an invention of an author of the seventh- [*sic*] century B.C.E. or later since the writer must have had records of some sort".[71] In contrast to earlier practice during the New Kingdom, Sheshonq I's list shows that Egyptian military action in Canaan now included sites north of

[68]Dever 2001: 73.
[69]Dever 2001: 72–3.
[70]Mazar 2003: 92.
[71]Mazar 2007c: 124.

Jerusalem, sites such as Beth Horon and Gibeon. The Egyptians must have had a serious reason to alter their traditional military route in Canaan and the most likely reason for this would be the power that Solomon would have possessed.[72] Mazar refers to those sites mentioned in Sheshonq's list which have yielded occupation layers of the Iron Age IIA, namely Arad, the Negev Highland sites, Taanach, and Reḥov. He adds that for some of these sites, such as Arad and the Negev highland sites, "there is no alternative, but to attribute the Iron IIA occupation layers to the tenth century B.C.E., preceding Sheshonq's raid".[73]

So, Sheshonq took the road towards Jerusalem and the areas to its north in his invasion of Canaan because Jerusalem together with the areas under its rule actually comprised something that was larger than "just a remote village" that had to be reckoned with; the Middle Bronze Age towers guarding the Gihon spring, the stepped stone structure and "some other public buildings nearby" are a witness to this scenario.[74] Indeed, Hugh Williamson has very aptly pointed out that it would be odd if the Temple came later than Solomon's period and that it was erroneously ascribed to him; it is difficult to imagine that the origin of such an institution as the temple would have been manipulated. In fact, the Psalms testify that the traditions of the liturgy were shared between Israel and Judah; indeed, the title "God of Jacob" is found in Psalm 46, which is clearly a Zionist hymn.[75] It is highly significant that "we never once find a reference to the 'God of Judah' alongside the familiar 'God of Israel'. These conservative religious traditions testify to some sense of profound cultural unity that transcends the parochial political establishments."[76] Such considerations based on the evidence provided by the Hebrew Bible support the idea of a United Monarchy (albeit on a smaller scale than that pictured

[72]Mazar 2007c: 124.
[73]Mazar 2007c: 125.
[74]Williamson 2015: 6.
[75]Williamson 2015: 6.
[76]Williamson 2015: 7.

in the texts) and they tally with the archaeological (largely of a stratigraphic nature) evidence dealt with above.[77]

Actually, we now have even clearer and more securely dated archaeological evidence whereby a stratigraphic excavation supports the concept of a United Monarchy in ancient Israel during the tenth century BCE. I am referring to the "Governor's Residency" at Tel 'Eton which was used for a long time and which had no raised floors and for which it was therefore very difficult to pin down the foundation date. However, "a number of radiocarbon (^{14}C) dates from a foundation deposit and from the floors' make-up" showed that "the building was built already in the 10th century BCE".[78] In this regard it is interesting that "the youngest possible date for the construction, within the 2σ Calibrated Age Range, is 921 BCE, thus apparently ruling out any construction date which is later than the time of the United Monarchy (from the first half of the 10th century to around 930 BCE)".[79] It is important to note that there are various reasons as to why this result is secure and why the make-up of the floor for which there was a foundation deposit is neither residual nor earlier.[80]

---

[77]Another interesting piece of textual information regarding the United Monarchy that tallies with the archaeological evidence discussed in this chapter can be found in Josephus' *Contra Apion*. It was on the suggestion of Professor John Day (to whom I offer my thanks) that I consulted this work, where I found that Josephus underscores the antiquity of the Jews in stark contrast to today's minimalists as well as to the calumnies spread by his contemporaries. He had consulted the Greek historians Menander of Ephesus and Dius, as well as the public records of the Tyrians that they guarded with great care (Thackeray 1926: 163, 165, 205, 207). With specific reference to the building of the temple of Solomon in Jerusalem, Josephus cites Dius, who mentions the part that Hiram of Tyre had played in this project (*Contra Apion* I, 17, especially 113-115). He also refers (in a summary fashion) to Menander of Ephesus regarding the list of rulers in Tyre from Hiram down to the foundation of Carthage (*Contra Apion*, I, 18, 121-125). In the summary that Josephus gives us there is "some corruption in the figures for the individual reigns, which do not amount to the total here given [by Josephus]", who gives a number of 155 years and 8 months (Thackeray 1926: 213). According to my calculations, the total should be 161 years. This does not alter the fact that even on a mathematical minimalist reckoning the latest possible date for Solomon's temple would be c. 948 BCE, which practically falls in the middle of the tenth century BCE, the commonly accepted date for the united monarchy.

[78]Faust and Sapir 2018: 1.

[79]Faust and Sapir 2018: 10

[80]Faust and Sapir 2018: 11.

It is important to keep in mind here also the well-known Tel Dan inscription (ninth century BCE) that commemorates Hazael's victory over the kings of Israel and Judah and which seemingly mentions *bytdwd*. Numerous discussions have arisen around this archaeological artefact, and it is not my aim to get involved in this debate here. I am mentioning this inscription simply to indicate that it seems reasonable to interpret the phrase *bytdwd* either as referring to the Davidic dynasty in general "or, as is more likely in an Aramaic context, to the state of Judah headed by the Davidic dynasty".[81] The inscription shows that Judah was a state to be reckoned with during the ninth century BCE, and, since this state must have taken time to consolidate itself, the logical conclusion is to assume that it is highly likely that it was founded in the tenth century BCE.

The points discussed in this chapter show that before marshalling the results of archaeology either in favour of or against supporting the existence of certain events of biblical history (such as that of the United Monarchy), it is important to check whether or not the excavations in question were carried out according to the strict rules of stratigraphic excavation, and to refrain from claiming that certain historical periods did not exist simply because the archaeological evidence for them is not there, or not yet there. In addition, when the archaeological evidence is available, it is important not to interpret it in such a way that the argument is tantamount to arguing in circles—an interpretational trap that will be discussed in the next chapter.

---

[81]Knoppers 1997: 36.

5

Adducing the evidence: Without going round in circles

As discussed in the previous chapter, the finds retrieved in archaeological excavations are deemed to be reliable if the excavation in question was conducted according to the rules of stratigraphic excavation. And it is clear that the findings of biblical scholars are deemed reliable if they are the result of a correct application of the critical ways of reading the biblical text. So what about relating (when applicable) the results of critical biblical research with those of archaeological discoveries? In this case it is important to emphasize that in reality we are not comparing and/or contrasting the Bible with archaeology, but our interpretation of the biblical text with our interpretation of the archaeological data.[1] In this process it is crucial to avoid falling into the trap of circular argumentation, which in this case would see biblical scholars appealing to archaeologists and the latter appealing to the former in order

---

[1]De Vaux 1970: 78, writes "Archaeology does not confirm the text, which is what it is, it can only confirm the interpretation which we give it". It is clear that even archaeological data stand in need of interpretation (see Chapter 2). Hence, what we are really doing is comparing our interpretation of the biblical texts with our interpretation of the archaeological data.

to interpret certain artefacts, such as in the case of the biblical word *bāmāh* which, as has already been noted, is commonly translated as a "high place". While the term *bāmāh* will be discussed later on in this chapter, we can certainly agree on the principle that one cannot explain A in the light of B and then proceed to elucidate the latter in the light of the former—certainly not without having first provided the relevant solid evidence in each case.

However, when it comes to relating the biblical and the archaeological interpretations of the relevant data, in the first instance one has to avoid any sort of generalization. Indeed as G.H.R. Horsley wrote with reference to the contribution that the study of Greek inscriptions from Ephesus make to our understanding of the New Testament, "There are no short cuts. The latter do not get us beyond the level of generalisation: 'the inscriptions and papyri are useful to illustrate the NT' is the type of platitude to be avoided. Only by coming to close quarters with these texts individually will their potential be realised. This can be exciting work because new texts are being addressed, which in turn so often allow us to view old questions in a new light."[2] Moreover, it is also important to keep in mind the fact that historical criticism (which is crucial for a serious study of the biblical texts and for relating the results of biblical and archaeological research) has its own limitations. In Hebrew Bible studies, those who practice historical criticism are often unable to establish the relevant facts and they have to content themselves with hypotheses. This is fine in itself, as long as it is made very clear that hypotheses are not established facts. The same holds good for archaeological research: as already shown above in Chapter 2, it is crucial to distinguish between the data that were retrieved and their interpretation, since it is only when the latter is correct that facts are established. Short of a correct interpretation (supported by the evidence) we are in the realm of hypotheses. In this context, it is worthwhile citing what D. Harrington wrote with reference to biblical studies and to apply

[2]Horsley 1992: 168.

it also to archaeology, especially Biblical Archaeology: "The problem comes when hypotheses or speculations about the Bible are presented and accepted as established facts on the grounds that 'scholars say'. Those who practice historical criticism and those who rely on it need to be aware of the limitations of historical detective work and acknowledge them publicly."[3]

The foregoing points mean that we have to proceed carefully and to take each case on its own merits in all the three phases that go to make up Biblical Archaeology, namely the study of the biblical texts, that of the archaeological evidence pertinent to them, and that of the relationship between our interpretation of the latter with that of the former. Indeed, Baruch Halpern was correct when he compared the study of Israel's historiography to the two gangs of workmen who dug out the Siloam tunnel in Jerusalem. As is well known, the two groups dug the tunnel from two different ends (approximately on a north–south axis) and met in the middle—as the Siloam Tunnel inscription testifies.[4] For Halpern, scholars dealing with the historiography of Israel too should work from two ends: the literary and the historical.[5] Where the literary and historical studies do not meet, "or where one works from one end only, tortuous and solipsistic analysis results".[6] This does not mean that scholars do not have their own biases. Indeed, these can be taken on board—as long as we remember that "perhaps a measured, dispassionate judgment characterizes the best history" but that "historiography can defend high principles in a setting of high charge".[7]

[3]Harrington 2012: 94.
[4]Gibson 1971: 21–3.
[5]In view of the aforementioned remarks in this chapter on the aims of archaeological research, the present author includes archaeology within the historical approach that Halpern mentions since archaeology too aims to tell a story about our ancestors. Indeed, archaeology can be viewed as a "specialized form of history" (Woodhead 1985: 10).
[6]Halpern 1996: 200.
[7]Halpern 1996: 11.

I shall now present two types of examples: the first type providing clear results, with the second type leaving us in the realm of uncertainty or of hypotheses at best. The first type consists of two examples, both dealing with toilets and/or the remains in them.

Between December 2015 and February 2016 S. Ganor and I. Kreimerman directed excavations in the southern part of the six-chambered gate at Tel Lachish that yielded the eighth-century BCE remains of a shrine in which there were, *inter alia*, two horned-altars. Seven of the horns (out of a total of eight) seem to have been deliberately cut off since they had been "truncated with a sharp tool",[8] and above the inner holy area of the shrine there was a toilet installed that consisted of a stone with a hole in its centre. In fact, in the western part of the small southern room of the eastern chamber of the gate there was a plastered floor cut by a pit in which there was "a meticulously hewn square stone (0.39 × 0.50 × 0.56m)" that had a round hole in its centre from which there issued a channel and which Ganor and Kreimerman correctly interpret as being "probably a toilet"; their interpretation is buttressed by similar toilets that had been discovered in Israel and Transjordan.[9] They interpret the overall archaeological remains as a sign of a deliberate desecration of the holy area: setting a toilet right over a shrine shows a deliberate intent to desecrate it, thus putting it out of action as far as its holy function is concerned. We have biblical evidence for this practice from 2 Kgs 10:27, which says that when Jehu destroyed the temple of Baal in Samaria he "made it a latrine to this day".[10] Since the remains in question date from the eighth century BCE, Ganor and Kreimerman think that the evidence can be interpreted as a result of King Hezekiah's religious reform (see 2 Kgs 18:4). Their excavations are the first to confirm the aforementioned practice, and which thus provide the evidence that turns out to be a concrete example

---

[8]Ganor and Kreimerman 2018.
[9]Ganor and Kreimerman 2018.
[10]Gray 2016.

and illustration of the information given in 2 Kgs 10:27. They correctly state that "the shrine had been desecrated and converted into a latrine, and the entrance to the inner sanctum was sealed. This is the first evidence in Israel of the destruction of a shrine in this manner."[11]

Another example of the first type discussed in this chapter, where the results of archaeological and biblical research tally in a context where the pertinent evidence is adduced and where there are no circular arguments involved, is provided by archaeoparasitology[12] and biblical research with reference to the last days of Jerusalem before its destruction by the Babylonians in 586 BCE. An examination of the contents of a toilet from Jerusalem dating to the early sixth century BCE indicates that the diet of the inhabitants consisted of "mustard, radishes, cabbage, parsley, coriander, and the like", namely of "backyard plants" and that some people suffered with tapeworm and whipworm.[13] Human beings will have these two parasites in their intestines "as a result of unsanitary and unhygienic conditions and practices—such as using human manure as fertilizer, not having enough water for thorough rinsing, and not having enough fuel to cook meat thoroughly".[14] Such an environmental scenario tallies perfectly with that depicted in various biblical texts with reference to the eighteen-month siege of Jerusalem by the Babylonians that led to its destruction in 586 BCE.[15] The biblical texts in question are very clear about the highly desperate situation that the Jerusalemites were in, to the extent that "the hands of compassionate women" had "boiled their own children; they became their food" (Lam. 4:10).[16]

[11]Ganor and Kreimerman 2018; Gray 2016.

[12]Archaeoparasitology is "the discipline that focuses on the relationships between behavior, environment, and parasite infection", and a discipline "developed from the need for a fine-tuned analysis of prehistoric ecological and behavioral conditions to assess the factors that affected disease" (Reinhard and Araújo 2008: 495).

[13]Cline 2009: 53.

[14]Cline 2009: 53.

[15]Cline 2009: 53.

[16]See also Lam. 2:20; 4:10; and Ezek. 5:10-17.

The relevant archaeological evidence consists of two "fine toilet seats" (each of which consisted of a large block of local limestone that was set in the floor over a cesspit) that were found in situ; "at least one of them was clearly in use at the time of the Babylonian destruction of the city [Jerusalem] in 586 B.C.E.".[17] The overall focus of the excavations in question was the period spanning the seventh and sixth centuries BCE. The toilet seat that was in use at the time of the Babylonian siege of Jerusalem was found in a location designated as Area G. An examination of the soil deposits in the cesspits below both toilet seats showed two important things. Firstly, it transpired that the faecal material was accompanied by "calcareous ash", indicating that the inhabitants of the city were doing their best to enhance sanitation and to reduce bacteria and fungus.[18] Secondly, the parasitological analysis specifically showed that the Jerusalemites suffered from whipworm infection due to either lack of hygiene, or to "limited availability of water for washing hands and produce".[19] The scientists also found tapeworm parasites in the faecal samples that they examined, something that could have been due to "the consumption of poorly cooked, perhaps raw, beef or pork, the only meats that carry this parasite".[20] It would have been particularly interesting in this regard to discover whether the tapeworm parasites in question ultimately stemmed from beef or pork since, if they had originated from the latter, this would show what a truly desperate situation the besieged Jerusalemites were in. Eating pork, alongside "boiling their own children" (Lam. 4:10), as already pointed out above, would clearly indicate the severity of the captives' plight. Unfortunately, at the time when the aforementioned analysis was done it was not possible for scientists to distinguish between the two species of tapeworm (*Taenia*) that can "infect

---

[17]Cahill et al. 1991: 64.

[18]Cahill et al. 1991: 67.

[19]Cahill et al. 1991: 69. It is important to note that the whipworm could also indicate "an infection arising either from the ingestion of fecally contaminated foods or from insanitary living arrangements in which people came into contact with human excrement" (ibid.). Either way, it is clear how dramatic the situation in the besieged city of Jerusalem was.

[20]Cahill et al. 1991: 69.

humans", namely *T. solium*, which stems from "raw or undercooked" pork, and *T. saginata*, which is a parasite that infects humans who eat "raw or under-cooked" beef.[21] Be that as it may, the foregoing results of archaeoparasitology that come from the analysis of relevant data from archaeological strata in Jerusalem dating to the period of the siege of Jerusalem by the Babylonians are sufficient to show how the scenario depicted in the Hebrew Bible is wholly buttressed by modern archaeological research.

I now turn to the second type of example where, in contrast to the previous two examples, there is no clarity with respect to what a particular type of archaeological artefact really looks like. I am specifically referring to what is known in the Hebrew Bible as a *bāmāh*, and for which there is no clear under-standing neither from the archaeological perspective nor from that of biblical research, and much less so from the sphere of Biblical Archaeology. Indeed, more often than not, when it comes to the *bāmāh* there are in fact a number of circular arguments involved, rather than the presentation of evidence which would allow scholars to integrate in a correct manner the biblical and archaeo-logical interpretation of the data. Let us start with the lexical aspect.

The standard dictionaries assign various meanings to the word *bāmāh*. Thus, for example, according to F. Brown, S.R. Driver, and C.A. Briggs, this word has three basic meanings: (1) high place, mountain; (2) high places, battlefields; and (3) high places as places of worship. This latter meaning refers to various places of worship, such as those found on high hills or mountains, under green trees, in cities, and those that consist of artificial mounds or platforms or that consist of chapels erected on these places of worship. Brown,

---

[21]Email from Dr Patrik Flammer to me dated 13th December 2016. The reason why it is was not possible to distinguish between the two species of *Taenia* is that these can only be distinguished via a "genetic identification" (since an identification is "not possible from the microscopic pictures"), which at the time the authors of the article Cahill et al. had not supplied. That is not surprising, however, "since genetic identification is still not widely used (as it is quite difficult) and the authors probably did not have appropriate facilities or specialists at their disposal" (email from Dr Patrik Flammer, 21st March 2017).

Driver, and Briggs list one instance (Ezek. 16:16) where they believe that *bāmāh* stands for a portable sanctuary.[22] L. Koehler, W. Baumgartner, and J.J. Stamm list four basic meanings for this word, namely back, hill, a (Canaanite) grave, and a high place/place of worship.[23] With respect to the term's occurrence (in its plural form, *bāmôt*) in Ezek. 16:16, they think that in this instance the basic idea is that of height linked with a bed or a couch and they refer to a study by O. Eissfeldt to support their translation of *bāmôt ṭluʾôt* as "colourful high couches" for use in cultic prostitution. The overall idea is parallel to that found in Isa. 57:7ff., where instead of *bāmôt* we find *miškāb*.[24] However, it should be pointed out that T.J. Lewis holds that in Isa. 57:7, as in Isa. 57:2, *miškāb* does not mean bed or couch, but tomb. This meaning "is attested in biblical texts and extra-biblical inscriptions".[25] All this goes to show how difficult it is to comprehend what *bāmāh* really means. Indeed, the traditional rendering of this word as "height"/"high place" is very old, but from the very beginning it was not that clear what it really meant. Thus, although in general the Septuagint version renders the word *bāmāh* as *hypsēlon*, whilst the Vulgate translates it as *excelsus*, there are times when the Septuagint gives various translations for it, such as "grave", "mound", "idol", "standing stone", and "altar". Moreover, there are also cases in the Septuagint when the word *bāmāh* "is simply transliterated, indicating possible uncertainty even in antiquity".[26]

The foregoing points help us to understand better why modern scholars (philologists as well as archaeologists) have spilled so much ink on the word *bāmāh*. Although there is no consensus as to what it really means, and therefore what type of artefact one is expected to exhibit if one claims that one has unearthed a *bāmāh*, it is worthwhile to try and see what the

[22]Brown, Driver, and Briggs 1906: 119.
[23]Koehler, Baumgartner, and Stamm 1994: 136.
[24]Koehler, Baumgartner, and Stamm 1994: 137 and references there.
[25]Lewis 2002: 178 n. 30.
[26]Coote 2007: 824.

original meaning of the word was and how it generally came to be used in the Hebrew Bible. A close reading of Mic. 3:12 shows that most probably the word *bāmāh* carried an original semantic meaning to do with a topographical feature, namely one that supports the translation of this word by "height" or "mountain".[27] It is a commonplace that eventually in the multiple religious contexts of the Hebrew Bible, *bāmāh* came to mean a "high place". However, no one knows exactly what such a "high place" looks like; the problem is one of circular arguments. Indeed, as Z. Zevit writes, "the casual way that different archaeologists use this word [*bāmāh*] to label various types of finds is based on Humpty-Dumpty philology: a word means exactly what I want it to mean".[28] Zevit highlights four meanings of *bāmāh/bāmôt* that scholars generally find for these words in the biblical texts. Thus, *bāmôt* shared "certain features" with altars without being altars as such; a *bāmāh* could also indicate a platform, or, as Zevit claims, it could also be something that could be covered by garments (see Ezek. 16:15-23) and which could also function as a pedestal for images; it could also be something the size of a small bed onto which one could go up to or ascend (see Jer. 48:35). Finally, Zevit also reminds us that according to the biblical texts a temple could be built over a *bāmāh* and that the latter is also found used in parallel to the temple sheltering the ark.[29] It is clear that the whole issue is unclear, to say the least. Thus, for example, when discussing cult sites that are less elaborate than temples and where God is viewing an offering made in his house, B.A. Levine writes: "or, at less elaborate cult-sites, he [the deity] is outside on a platform (*bāmâ*) or the like, situated near the altar".[30] The words "or the like" are sufficient to show how uncertain the meaning of *bāmāh* actually is.

---

[27]Gelston 2010: 102*.
[28]Zevit 2001: 262.
[29]Zevit 2001: 262-3 and references there.
[30]Levine 2002: 133-4.

The points discussed thus far suffice to show that when it comes to the religious semantic field of the word *bāmāh*, the common factors that cut across the multiple meanings that scholars ascribe to it are that it is a sanctuary, albeit without our knowing exactly how it looks in practice. Amos 7:9 constitutes the biblical kick-off point for this meaning of *bāmāh*, seeing that it is clear that in this instance *bāmôt* ("high places") parallels *miqd^{e}šēy* ("sanctuaries of") thus rendering these two words closely related, being used in a composition type known as "synonymous parallelism".[31] The reason that "high place" and "sanctuary" are synonymous is that it seems to be a universal phenomenon for societies to link God's presence with mountains, and thus with heights; indeed this obtains also in the Hebrew Bible, for example, in Ps. 121:1.[32] The above-mentioned original aspect of height present in the word *bāmāh* and its development to the point of signifying "sanctuary" thus become clear; indeed, "from biblical and archaeological data, the meaning of the Hebrew word *bâmāh* can be further extended to include 'height, hill, mound, a projecting mass of rock, and a stone burial cairn'".[33] P.H. Vaughan accepted the idea that *bāmāh* means "sanctuary" as in Amos 7:9, but he also thought that it could signify a "cultic platform". He adduced 1 Kgs 14:23 to support his claim.[34] However, the original text does not warrant this interpretation and it thus seems best to accept "sanctuary" as the basic meaning of *bāmāh* when it is used in a religious context. Numbers 33:52b supports this understanding. It states: "and you will destroy all their metal statues, and you will demolish all *bāmōtām*". The latter word is generally translated as "their high places", though the context as well as the parallelism with "their metal statues" indicates that it would be better to render it by "their sanctuaries" in view of the fact that statues are normally placed in sanctuaries.

---

[31]Kennedy and Freedman 1963: 383; Vaughan 1974: 13.

[32]Kennedy and Freedman 1963: 383.

[33]Kennedy and Freedman 1963: 383.

[34]Vaughan 1974: 12–13.

The *Jewish Study Bible*[35] wholly supports the foregoing conclusions. This is borne out, for example, by the manner in which it renders *bāmôt haśśᵉ'ārîm* in 2 Kgs 23:8. It translates this phrase as "the shrines of the gates" in contrast with multiple modern translations that render it as "the high places of the gates". The *Jewish Study Bible* also supplies a good explanation for the phrase "the shrines of the gates" by stating that such shrines "have been excavated at Dan, Tirzah, and Geshur (an Aramaean city near the northeast shore of the Sea of Galilee). They consisted of a small area in which one or more standing stones were set up."[36] Such a depiction of what a gate shrine could look like is good, but it should be noted that B.S.J. Isserlin is more cautious with respect to some alleged examples, including that from Tirzah, since the basin and the uncertain example of a pillar set in an open area in the gate at this site could also be interpreted as "an olive-crushing plant".[37] He also considers the alleged examples of gate sanctuaries from Beersheba as well as a "possible religious structure" in an open area between the inner and outer gates at Tel Dan, and in both cases he concludes that these two examples too are unconvincing.[38] However, he interprets other data from the outer gate at Dan as actually turning out to be the best candidate for a gate sanctuary when he considers the "five standing stones" set against the wall of this gate in front of which there was a "stone bench or table", apparently for offerings. The dishes for incense burning, oil lamps, and pottery bowls from nearby corroborate Isserlin's choice of these remains as constituting a good example of a gate sanctuary.[39]

J.T. Whitney has pointed out that the word *bāmāh* (or its plural form *bāmôt*) occurs ten times in 2 Kings 23.[40] Despite the fact that it actually occurs

---

[35]Berlin and Brettler 2004.
[36]Berlin and Brettler 2004: 772–3.
[37]Isserlin 1998: 245.
[38]Isserlin 1998: 245–6.
[39]Isserlin 1998: 246.
[40]Whitney 1979: 136–8.

nine times—in vv. 5, 8 (twice), 9, 13, 15 (twice), 19, and 20[41]—it is interesting to note that, in this one chapter, *bāmāh/bāmôt* actually refers to various kinds of sanctuaries. In vv. 5, 8 (first occurrence), and 9 it refers to shrines outside Jerusalem, whilst in v. 8 (second occurrence) the reference is to the "shrines of the gates". In v. 15 the ancient Canaanite shrine at Bethel is labelled as a *bāmāh*, whereas in vv. 19 and 20 the reference is to the shrines in Samaria. 2 Kings 23 shows us that *bāmāh* can refer to various types of shrines, which leads us to conclude that it is best to equate this word with "shrine" and then to allow the context to specify what type of shrine it is actually referring to.

Thus, when the semantic field of the word *bāmāh* is a religious one, it is highly probable that it is referring to a cultic site, and thus it would be best translated by the word "shrine", as already pointed out above. In view of the points discussed in the preceding paragraph, it is clear that when it comes to pinning down a *bāmāh* in the archaeological record it is virtually impossible to do so. The reason is that the "shrine" in question could be of various types, as 2 Kings 23 shows. In essence, a *bāmāh* is a cultic site that by the sixth century BCE took the form of a small shrine. Indeed, the archaeological record indicates (if we accept that *bāmāh* is best translated by the word "shrine") that the real difference between a *bāmāh* and a *hêkāl* is that of size. This allows us to conclude that a *bāmāh* is a shrine that is smaller than a *hêkāl*, which is usually translated as "temple".

The *overall* evidence supplied in the Hebrew Bible is that a *bāmāh* typically took the form of "a permanent multi-roomed building in an established settlement".[42] The vast majority of the *bāmôt* were located within settled areas. While they are often linked with worship "upon every high hill and under

---

[41]The reason why Whitney says that *bāmāh* occurs ten times in 2 Kgs 23 is because he also includes v. 10, where the Topheth is mentioned. Whitney is aware that in this verse the Topheth is not called a *bāmāh* but he appeals to the fact that in the "contemporary Jeremiah" it is thus called (Whitney 1979: 138). This is correct, but such a stance does not allow us to count v. 10 as actually using the word *bāmāh*.

[42]Coote 2007: 824.

every green tree" (so Jer. 2:20), this is actually based "on sparse attestation".[43] W.B. Barrick too is of the opinion that the syntax used in connection with the word *bāmāh* shows "that one does not climb up a *bamah*, but rather one climbs up *to* a *bamah*".[44] Indeed, *babbāmôt* would best be translated as "in" the *bāmôt*, since a *bāmāh* "is something within which cultic acts were performed—not a piece of cultic furniture (like a platform or altar), but an installation within which cultic furniture could be housed and used".[45]

While the foregoing conclusions are correct, it is important to keep in mind the fact that they are true with respect to the *overall* evidence that is presented in the Hebrew Bible. This is so, especially in view of the fact, for example, that, although the preposition *bēt* typically means "in", or is used in connection with motion "in" or "into" a place, it also possesses "many other meanings: *on, against, with, by, for*".[46] J.C.L. Gibson reminds us that, when it comes to the basic meaning of "in" or of motion "into" a place of the preposition *bēt*, we need to keep in mind the difference between its usage in Hebrew and in English. Thus, the *bēt* of presence translates into English as that of presence *in* a house but presence *at* a place. In this case, the preposition is referring to a static scenario that is in contrast to the dynamic aspect, and thus to one that refers to motion "into" somewhere.[47] Moreover, *bēt* can in fact also mean "on" or "upon", such as in Num. 23:2.[48] Indeed, there are clear examples of this usage of *bēt*: "*on* the altar" (Gen. 8:20); "*on* the necks of the camels" (Judg. 8:21); "*on* his loins" (1 Kgs 2:25); "a helmet *on* his head" (Isa. 59:17); "his blood be *upon* him" (Lev. 20:9); and

---

[43]Coote 2007: 824.

[44]Barrick 1980: 53.

[45]Barrick 1980: 54, where he himself also notes that Isa. 16:12 might constitute the only exception that would allow us to view the *bāmāh* as something upon which one could go. However, he correctly points out that it would be dangerous to go by this one example since Isa. 16:12 is a problematic text where *'al* could mean "at" and *'el* could signify "in" as in Isa. 28:22.

[46]Joüon and Muraoka 2006: 457.

[47]Gibson 1994: 146.

[48]Gibson 1994: 149.

"his blood be *upon* his head" (Josh. 2:19).[49] This should thus make us wary before totally excluding such a meaning of the preposition *bēt* in the phrase *babbāmôt*, which could thus be translated as "on the *bāmôt*" in certain contexts. Vaughan had already correctly noted that in 1 Kgs 3:4 the word *bāmāh* referred to an altar, seeing that it was clearly used as a synonym for this latter word which is preceded by the preposition *'al*, namely "upon"; moreover, as just noted, in Num. 23:2 the word "altar" is preceded by *bēt* with the unambiguous meaning of "upon/on".

All this would bring us back to square one, namely that in reality we do not have an unequivocal meaning of the word *bāmāh* in the Hebrew Bible. As shown above, it seems that, when carrying a semantic value related to religion, it generally means "shrine" though at other times it could also mean "altar".[50] J.T. Whitney reminds us that the Mesha Stela[51] (in line 3) provides "the only non-biblical reference" to the word *bāmāh* whose semantic field is cultic, namely when it refers to a "shrine". In this case, we are told that King Mesha of Moab built a shrine (*bāmāh*) in Karchoh for the god Kemosh.[52] Be that as it may, the point is that we cannot *a priori* be certain what a *bāmāh* is really referring to in each text where it occurs, the upshot being that we do not know what a *bāmāh* should actually look like. As Whitney aptly says, *bāmôt* were "different things in different places at different times".[53] Moreover it is important to keep in mind the fact that the various biblical references (such as in 1 Kgs 14:23; 2 Kgs 16:4; and 2 Chron. 28:4) to the *bāmôt* that were "on every high hill and under every spreading tree" should be viewed as a case of

---

[49]Brown, Driver, and Briggs 1906: 89.

[50]Davies 2002: 274–5; Schmidt 2006: 315.

[51]The Mesha Stela (also known as the Moabite Stone) is a ninth-century BCE inscription that Mesha, king of Moab, had engraved in Moabite (a West Semitic tongue very close to Classical Hebrew) on a large piece of basalt. Amongst other things, Mesha mentions his victorious dealings with the descendants of King Omri of the Northern Kingdom of Israel.

[52]Whitney 1979: 135.

[53]Whitney 1979: 147.

the literary device of merismus,[54] and that therefore in fact *bāmôt* "were to be found everywhere".[55]

The foregoing points still leave us stranded when it comes to our trying to understand what a *bāmāh* is when we attempt to marshal any relevant archaeological evidence for it. Even if we accept that in general when used in a cultic sense *bāmāh* refers to a shrine, or at other times to an altar, we are left with the problem of not knowing what the altars and shrines in question actually look like. J.A. Emerton accepts that *bāmôt* often referred to local sanctuaries, but he too thinks that we do not have enough information that allows us to know the necessary details, and, as he says, "perhaps the wisest policy is to regard any local sanctuary as possibly a *bāmâ* but to recognize that we cannot be certain".[56] The problem becomes even more acute when we keep in mind the fact that archaeologists do not always have clear-cut criteria that allow them to decide what constitutes a space as sacred.

M.D. Coogan has come up with four criteria that would allow archaeologists to read the relevant data as cultic. He first mentions "isolation" in the sense of a separation of the sacred and the profane, something indicated architecturally via a "temenos wall".[57] However, how would this criterion apply in the case of a *bāmāh* when it is found in an open area? The second criterion is that of "exotic materials", in the sense that "the special function of cultic sites, will normally result in the presence of material not typical of other contexts, such as miniature vessels".[58] I think that we should be wary of this criterion since the foregoing statement could lead us to fall prey to labelling as cultic what cannot be deciphered as belonging to any other known category.

[54]Merismus is a figure of speech that uses two opposite terms (for example, "day and night") to indicate the two terms themselves and everything else lying between them. Hence, "day and night" would signify all the time.

[55]Whitney 1979: 136.

[56]Emerton 1997: 129. Note that Emerton accepts that *bāmāh* could in fact refer to a temple, to an altar, or even to a cultic platform (Emerton 1997: 121–3, 123–4, and 123 respectively).

[57]Coogan 1987: 2.

[58]Coogan 1987: 2.

In the third place, Coogan mentions the criterion of "continuity", namely the use of spaces that were used for cultic purposes across large tracts of time.[59] Finally, he invokes "parallels", namely plans, altars, pedestals and so on that are parallel "to cultic installations known from written or non-written sources".[60] These four criteria function only as indicators; archaeologists cannot apply them mechanically. They have to be used in a flexible manner, and, as Coogan himself writes, "none of these criteria, of course, is watertight; they overlap in some ways, and the absence of one or more (especially that of continuity for one-period sites) is not necessarily conclusive. But the higher the number of criteria present the more probable is the assignment of a cultic function."[61]

The upshot of the discussion on the word *bāmāh* is that in reality philologists have not come up with an unequivocal meaning for it, which thus explains why archaeologists cannot pin down this "artefact" in the archaeological record beyond any reasonable doubt. In brief: archaeologists have not in fact discovered any clear-cut examples of *bāmôt*. Scholars have made various proposals as to what a *bāmāh* would look like. The not-so-uncommon trend to identify platforms as cultic and label them as *bāmôt* is incorrect; as Fowler states in connection with Vaughan's stance regarding the latter's idea that *bāmôt* could also very well be truncated or low oblong cones: "this is simply untrue! Archaeology, here, has provided sure examples not of *bāmôt* but of one scholar's interpretation of the phenomenon".[62] Isserlin has rightly challenged the idea that a *bāmāh* could also be a cairn monument. It is highly unlikely that this is a correct explanation of what a *bāmāh* is since "the close juxtaposition of such monuments [cairns] and the short duration of their use argues against their interpretation as *bamahs*, but further investigation is needed to establish their true character".[63] The above-mentioned idea that

---

[59]Coogan 1987: 3.
[60]Coogan 1987: 3.
[61]Coogan 1987: 3.
[62]Fowler 1982: 211 and references there.
[63]Isserlin 1998: 248.

a *bāmāh* is often a sanctuary is fine in itself, but the problem for its identification in the archaeological record arises in an acute manner when we realize that scholars have made the following main four proposals for its archaeological identification as linked with a cult: a temple, an altar, an open-air cultic site, and a platform for rituals.[64] The issue is further compounded when we keep in mind the fact that we do not have one excavated site to which the Hebrew Bible refers with the word *bāmāh*.[65] Incorrect identifications of *bāmôt* in the archaeological record have been made, with the so-called Conway High Place at Petra being the most notorious example. I already discussed in detail above in Chapter 2 how Peter Parr has shown beyond any reasonable doubt that the remains in question at this site did not constitute a *bāmāh* at all. His accurate analysis of the data showed that the structure is best identified as a military fortress and that it is therefore more appropriate to speak of the Conway Tower rather than of the Conway High Place. There is no religious structure at all in this case, but a military one dating to the late Hellenistic/early Roman period in Jordan.[66]

At present we are not in a position where archaeologists can appeal to the philologists of the Hebrew Bible and vice versa in order to identify a clear-cut example of a *bāmāh* in the archaeological record and a crystal-clear meaning of this word in the Hebrew Bible. If such an appeal were to be made, that would be tantamount to arguing in circles. The case of the *bāmāh* is just one example of how careful we need to be when we seek to integrate our interpretations of the written with that of the non-written evidence. Indeed, as D.R. Ap-Thomas stated, "given our present very incomplete knowledge of what a bamah really was and looked like, we need to find an edifice actually labelled 'bamah' before we can be sure".[67]

---

[64]Nakhai 1994: 21.
[65]Emerton 1997: 128.
[66]Parr 1962: 64, 77–8.
[67]Ap-Thomas 1975: 167.

However, when it comes to integrating the biblical and the relevant archaeological evidence in connection with certain historical events, not everything is doom and gloom. Thus, for example, the analysis of the residues of the faecal remains found in the sixth-century BCE toilets in Jerusalem by the emerging discipline of archaeoparasitology offers a clear example of this. As shown above, we now know how very real the biblical picture of the desperate situation of the besieged Jerusalemites was. Archaeoparasitology is now making important contributions to historical research,[68] and it is thus important for archaeologists of the southern Levant to be on the lookout for toilets and the faecal residues in them so that this discipline will be able to contribute also to our knowledge of the history of ancient Israel.

It is commonly taken for granted that the contribution that archaeology can make to biblical studies is in essence by way of illustrating the cultural and historical *background* of many biblical texts. However, as I shall discuss in the next chapter, there is also a sense in which archaeology can make a *direct* contribution to the text of the Bible (both in the sense of textual criticism as well as in the semantic field of the text), besides the fact that at times it is the Bible that can throw light on archaeological conundrums.

---

[68]There are now novel approaches in the discipline of archaeoparasitology that allow molecular identification of parasites. The examination of samples from Lübeck allowed scholars to distinguish between the two species of *Taenia*—in this case "the source of human Taenia infection was most likely from undercooked beef because the sequences that were obtained matched the beef tapeworm T. saginata rather than the pork tapeworm T. solium" (Flammer et al. 2018: 6, 2). Unfortunately, such a distinction between beef and pork for the *Taenia* samples from Jerusalem mentioned above (see n. 21) was not possible. However, the contribution of archaeoparasitology to historical studies could be of great import now, seeing, for example, that for medieval Lübeck it allowed scholars to affirm that the results obtained were "consistent with its importance as a Hanseatic trading centre. Collectively, these results introduce molecular archaeoparasitology as an artefact-independent source of historical evidence" (ibid.: 1).

6

In practice:
A two-way flow of traffic—
archaeology⇌Bible

The preceding chapters have illustrated the basic criteria that biblical scholars would do well to keep in mind when assessing the results of archaeological research. Grasping these basic criteria is not difficult, though there are cases when problems can arise *in practice* when scholars attempt to relate the results of archaeology to those of biblical research or vice versa. Indeed, it will become apparent that often one has to start *in medias res* whilst sticking to the canons of interpretation of each discipline, in this case those of archaeology and of biblical exegesis. It will fast become apparent that the cases like those discussed in the previous chapters, though the most frequent, are definitely not the only ones. Although it is a commonplace that archaeology throws a good deal of light on the Bible by way of illustrating its cultural and historical background, it is also true that there are cases when it actually makes a direct contribution to the text itself, either by way of settling issues of textual criticism or by way of throwing light on the semantics of the biblical text. Moreover, there could be cases when it is the biblical text that actually throws light on a problem that arises from the data that archaeologists unearth. Thus, we actually witness a two-way flow of traffic: with archaeology illuminating the Bible, and the latter helping us solve certain archaeological conundrums. I shall provide various examples of this exchange in the present chapter.

Kurtis Peters has done an excellent job of underscoring the fact that in the field of semantics meaning is not only a part of the language system, and that "the quest for meaning must take the conceptual world of the language users into account".[1] Since concepts are linked to an "extra-linguistic context", short of talking to the native speakers (something which we cannot do, obviously, in the case of ancient Israel), one excellent way of getting at the relevant conceptual world is to make use of the results of archaeology. Thus, with respect to "a study of cooking in Biblical Hebrew", for example, it is "likely that the most fruitful information for providing such [extra-linguistic] context would be archaeology of cooking environments in ancient Israel".[2] Dictionaries give us the basic information "to distinguish the sense of one word from some others", whilst an encyclopaedic view "will attempt to account for all information related to the sense of that word".[3] Archaeology (including ethnoarchaeology) provides an excellent gateway to the encyclopaedic knowledge that we need in order to fully grasp the physical realities evoked by the words used in the languages of ancient societies, including those pertinent to the biblical world. In short, lexemes cannot be equated with concepts—the latter include much more than just lexemes.[4] Some examples will clarify how archaeology helps us to grasp much better the semantics of Biblical Hebrew.

---

[1]Peters 2016: 18.
[2]Peters 2016: 21–2.
[3]Peters 2016: 43 and references there.
[4]Peters 2016: 205.

In the Hebrew Bible, the verb *'ûg* is found only once, in Ezek. 4:12. Peters translates the verse in question thus: "You shall eat it as a barley-cake, baking it in their sight on human dung". The basic concept for the verb *'ûg* is that of creating something related to food (in this case an *'ugâ*). Archaeology and philological analysis help us to better understand this basic concept. The Septuagint version employs the verb *egkrúptō* and the cognate accusative *egkruphías*, thus showing "that, at least to the mind of the Greek translator, there was a practice of concealment involved in this baking activity".[5] Ethnoarchaeology provides "comparative ethnographic evidence" that "could feasibly link this language to the practice of the Bedouin who use the *tabun*[6] outside of the living space" and who put the fuel "on top of and around" it. They then bury this oven in "embers and ashes", and when it is sufficiently hot the Bedouin will pull back the fuel until they reveal the opening of the oven, allowing them to place their cakes inside. They then recover the oven with embers until the cakes are cooked. The Septuagint version of Ezek. 4:12 together with the ethnoarchaeological information just described help us to comprehend the concept behind this biblical verse: Ezekiel piles human dung on an oven baking the bread (barley-cake) *inside* it.[7]

By employing cognitive grammar[8] in his analysis of the text of the Hebrew Bible, Peters has succeeded in cutting through the difficulties that the verb *bāšal* has posed for many scholars. Via his meticulous study of the background necessary to properly comprehend this verb, Peters concludes that: "there is

---

[5]Peters 2016: 125.

[6]The *tabun* is one of the two types of clay ovens commonly found in excavations on ancient Near Eastern sites. The other type of oven (also of clay) is called the *tannur*. This latter type is larger and is partly dug into the ground, reaching a height of c. 1 m and having a diameter of c. 40–60 cm. It was heated from the inside whilst the *tabun* was heated from the outside with the fuel placed against its outer surface. The *tabun* was smaller and reached a height of up to c. 30cm (Peters 2016: 81, 82, 87).

[7]Peters 2016: 125.

[8]Cognitive grammar is that branch of theoretical linguistics that seriously takes into account the viewpoint that "meaning resides in the mind and not in the language system itself nor in the world behind it. The mind, of course, employs the language system and interacts with the world around it, but the location of meaning nevertheless is in the mind. Meaning is cognitive" (Peters 2016: 139).

no need for linguistic laxity with this word. It is not maximally generic for cooking in general, nor does it mean 'roast' or 'bake' in any known occurrence. Rather it refers to cooking in liquid, plain and simple."[9] This result helps him to provide us with a clearer understanding of the semantics of 2 Sam. 13:1-22, the narrative about Amnon violating his sister Tamar. In this story Jonadab and Amnon use different cooking terms, but both of them indicate that the cooking is taking place at a location from which Amnon can view from his bed. The archaeology of ancient Israel teaches us that ovens were often located on the ground floor of houses, while also that there were "hearths upstairs in the living space".[10] Given this, Tamar could not have baked proper bread but "flat bread stretched across a hearth", and given the area where the cooking took place, neither could she have done anything that would have entailed "normal baking practices". Moreover, since a type of bread is in question, roasting is also excluded.[11] The verb *bāšal* here means "to boil", and boiling is something that could have been done on a hearth. Peters could reach these precise results because he integrated the cultural information about cooking practices in ancient Israel (gleaned from general archaeological and ethnoarchaeological research) with an analysis of the relevant textual data. This shows us how useful the employment of cognitive grammar is for an enhanced analysis of the biblical text since it clearly exemplifies the fact that "words can only be understood in tandem with the concepts they represent",[12] something which we can get at through careful archaeological investigation when ancient societies are involved.

Hosea 7:4-9 is a passage that certainly is not lacking in textual problems. These need not be rehearsed in full here. This passage provides us with a very significant opportunity to put in place the methodological conclusions

---

[9]Peters 2016: 205.
[10]Peters 2016: 192.
[11]Peters 2016: 196.
[12]Peters 2016: 51.

reached in the foregoing paragraph. Here I would like to underscore how information gained through archaeology could provide a solution to problems arising in the field of textual criticism. This passage deals with the anarchy that prevailed in the Northern Kingdom of Israel in the second half of the eighth century BCE and this is done via the imagery of baking. In v. 6, the word *ōpēhem* is problematic since it could either stem from the verb *ʾāpāh* ("to bake") or from the noun *ʾap* ("anger"). Peters opts for the former derivation, thus maintaining the Masoretic Text. Such an option is always the first and best approach in textual criticism (since a *lectio difficilior*, the most difficult reading, should be given priority). He translates *ōpēhem* as "their baker", although this form is "opaque" and it is best read as "being an example either of an unknown form (perhaps northern) or an example of the author's artistry".[13] In order to support his reading, Peters makes use of the knowledge that we have from archaeology and ethnoarchaeology regarding baking and food preparation. In v. 8 Ephraim is depicted like a cake that is not turned, and this image clearly reminds us of "baking over a fire" since we do know that "it is not easy to flip bread once it is inside the *tabun*, nor would it be entirely necessary".[14] It thus seems that the scenario is that of bread that is baked either directly over the coals or on a *saj*,[15] since in this case the bread that is not turned would simply be overcooked (and thus burned) on one side, whilst not being cooked on the other (top) side. Importantly, ethnoarchaeology led Peters to this conclusion, whilst he also makes use of comparative philology to throw light on the phrase *śybh zrqh bw* (v. 9), namely "grey hairs are sprinkled upon him". Here Peters refers to the Akkadian equivalent of this Hebrew phrase, which in tablet XI of the

---

[13]Peters 2016: 175, 174.
[14]Peters 2016: 175.
[15]The *saj* is a modern cooking utensil usually of metal and "shaped like a large bowl inverted on the fire" (Peters 2016: 84). Its archaeological equivalent is the ceramic baking trays with holes on their underside and which consisted of "large discs with a rim" and which "were likely placed directly on the fire" (Peters 2016: 84).

Epic of Gilgamesh means "to throw off mould/become mouldy".[16] Thus, the overall image of Ephraim in Hos. 7:4-9 "is one of a nation being consumed from all sides, both scorched and consumed by mould. However, as Hosea suggests, Ephraim is clueless to it all."[17]

Another clear example of how archaeology can make a direct contribution to the field of textual criticism comes from the New Testament. In Mark 10:25 we find the (in)famous word *kámēlon*, which is generally taken to mean "camel". The imagery here seems too stretched; it is not logical to visualize a camel passing through the eye of a needle, even if one wanted to employ hyperbole. The first thing to note is that there is no evidence for a gate in Jerusalem called Needle's Eye, through which a camel could be pictured as passing. The solution to the conundrum of the imagery in Mark 10:25 comes from Greek papyri unearthed in various excavations. Thanks to these inscriptions we know that there was a "widespread identification of simple vowels" which "led to manifold textual variants in the manuscript tradition [of first-century CE Palestine and thus of the New Testament writings too]".[18] This fact throws important light on the word *kámēlon* in Mark 10:25, since *kámilon* from *kámilos* ("a ship's hawser, a cable") and *kámēlon* ("camel") "would have been pronounced the same in first-century Palestine".[19] This means that we can safely read *kámilon* rather than *kámēlon* which makes more sense, since this "does not reduce the hyperbole of the saying of Jesus; it just makes it less illogical and grotesque".[20]

---

[16]Note that in Akkadian *šibtu(m)*, *inter alia*, means "greyness" (Black, George, and Postgate 2000: 370), and that in Tablet XI of the *Epic of Gilgamesh* we find this word with reference to a fifth portion of bread that, amongst other things, "had produced a (mouldy) stain" (*ši-ba it-ta-di* in line 228 and which appears as *ši-pa it-ta-di* in line 240, for which see George 2003b: 716–17, 718–19. It is clear that when bread has produced greyness it means that mould is to be found on it.

[17]Peters 2016: 175 and reference there.

[18]Gignac 1989: 44.

[19]Gignac 1989: 44.

[20]Gignac 1989: 44.

The foregoing practical examples of Biblical Archaeology have all shown (just as those discussed in the previous chapters did) how archaeology sheds important light on the Bible and that it does this in various ways, such as by elucidating important matters dealing with the relevant cultural and historical background of the biblical text or indeed even by highlighting problems of textual criticism directly. However, we do not have a situation involving a one-way stream of traffic, for there are instances where it is the biblical text that can help us to come to grips with outstanding problems that some of the data retrieved in excavations pose. In this regard, I shall dwell at length on the difficulties that some of the inscriptions unearthed at Kuntillet ʿAjrud (henceforth KA) and Khirbet el-Qôm (henceforth KQ) have presented for various scholars, especially for biblical specialists. In reality, I shall focus primarily on the data from KA and muster in those from KQ only when they are necessary for the present discussion.

It not my intention here to tackle the much-debated identification of the site of KA; for the purpose of this discussion it suffices to keep in mind that KA is generally accepted as being Israelite, "but with Judahite and Philistine ceramics and with some Phoenician script and pottery", a phenomenon which "seems to fit the organization of the international trade route between the Mediterranean and the Red Seas [*sic*] in the first half of the 8th century BCE".[21] This supports the idea that the site of KA functioned primarily as a caravanserai. Thus different groups of people visited the site, with some of them leaving behind numerous blessings and inscriptions in west Semitic.[22] There were inscriptions incised in stone, others written in ink on storage jars, whilst others were inscribed in red or black ink on wall plaster, with some of these latter inscriptions in the Phoenician script, though it is often claimed

---

[21]Lemaire 2016: 198–9.

[22]The vast majority of the inscriptions from KA are written in Hebrew. However, I use the words "west Semitic" for the inscriptions retrieved at this site in order to account for the fact that the inscriptions on the wall plaster are written in the Phoenician script, and, as discussed further on, are possibly drafted in the Phoenician tongue.

that the language used was Hebrew. The consensus is that all the inscriptions date to the end of the ninth century/beginning of the eighth century BCE.[23] It would seem that the inscriptions on the storage jars were scribal exercises and not letters since "no one sends a letter on a pithos".[24] As far as the inscriptions that were etched in Phoenician writing are concerned, it is logical to think that they were in fact written in the Phoenician tongue and not in the Hebrew language, since on *a priori* grounds this is "a simpler explanation" that allows us to envisage that Phoenician people "stayed or at least passed through Kuntillet 'Ajrud".[25] This would obviously fit well the function of KA as a type of caravanserai for people such as the Phoenicians, who engaged in international trade and who were expert in trade ventures, but it would lead us to consider the question as to how a Phoenician person would have invoked Yahweh (the God of Israel), as we find in inscription 4.1.1: "…by Yahweh of Teman and by his *asherah*…".[26] Does this mean that a Phoenician would have asked for a blessing by Yahweh, the god of Israel? In a syncretistic scenario, that would make sense.[27] However, we should also keep in mind the fact that the Phoenician script was used in the Northern Kingdom and there could very well have been an Israelite from the north who at KA wrote the aforementioned inscription in the Phoenician script.[28]

The difficulties that some of the inscriptions from KA have posed for biblical scholars are best illustrated by two inscriptions from the site, namely one on Pithos A and the other on Pithos B, which read respectively *brkt 'tkm lyhwh šmrn wl'šrth* ("I have blessed you by Yahweh of Samaria and by his *asherah*") and *brktk lyhwh tmn wl'šrth* ("I have blessed you by Yahweh

---

[23]Lemaire 2016: 197.
[24]Lemaire 2016: 202 and references there.
[25]Lemaire 2016: 205.
[26]Lemaire 2016: 205 and references there.
[27]Indeed, "it is, of course, not impossible that a Phoenician visitor used this divine name [Yahweh]" (Dijkstra 2001: 22).
[28]Dijkstra 2001: 22.

of Teman and by his *asherah*").[29] Biblical scholars find two things that are disturbing for them in these inscriptions. Firstly, the phrases "Yahweh of Samaria"/"Yahweh of Teman" are problematic because they fly in the face of the grammatical rule commonly recited in Biblical Hebrew classes—namely, that a definite noun (in this case a proper noun, Yahweh) cannot be in the construct state.[30] Secondly, and much more problematic, is the mention that someone is blessing another person by Yahweh and "his *asherah*". A number of biblical scholars prefer to translate this latter word by a common noun, namely "cultic pole"/"sacred tree", on the grounds that proper names (in this case the goddess Asherah) cannot take a pronominal suffix.[31] In reality even if the word "*asherah*" were to be translated as "cultic pole/sacred tree", it would still in fact constitute a reference to the Canaanite goddess Asherah (with the implication that Yahweh would have had a consort) since, as is well known, the tree is generally taken as the symbol of this goddess.

Are the two foregoing objections cast in stone, or does the overall evidence allow us to reach different conclusions? If the answer is "yes", would that really allow us to translate the above-mentioned storage jar inscriptions unambiguously? The first point regarding the rule that proper names cannot be in the construct state has in fact been tackled by various scholars with the result that we now know that in practice we do have evidence of proper names in the construct state. Thus, for example, in a footnote that consists of a revision and/or an update of the original text in question, Takamitsu Muraoka accepts

---

[29]The inscription on Pithos A is number 3.1, whilst that on Pithos B is number 3.6 in the *editio princeps* of the inscriptions from KA (Aḥituv, Eshel, and Meshel 2012: 87, 95). For a general overview of the inscriptions from KA (and KQ), see Dijkstra 2001: 14–44. For a discussion that includes observations on the form of the letters see Renz 1995: 47–64 (for the KA inscriptions) and Renz 1995: 202–11 (for the KQ inscriptions).

[30]See, for example, Joüon and Muraoka 2006: 451.

[31]Thus, for example, Gibson (1994: 34) says that "no proper names, place, divine or personal" can take a pronominal suffix. This leads him to conclude that, for example, in the above-mentioned inscription on Pithos A at KA the pronominal suffix in *wlʾšrth* is referring to Samaria and to be translated as "its", and the whole phrase as "by its 'sacred *place*/pole'" (ibid.).

the evidence for what it is and cites the phrases *yhwh šmrn* and *yhwh tmn* as instances of the fact that the divine name Yahweh can be in the construct state.[32] With reference to these two phrases, John Emerton would accept that the proper name Yahweh can be in the construct state when he writes: "in view of the pointing of *ăram* in the construct state in the phrase 'Aram-naharaim', it seems to me likely that *yhwh* is also in the construct state in such phrases [as *yhwh ṣebāʾ ôt*]".[33]

Although Emerton accepts that a proper name, such as the divine name Yahweh, can be in the construct state and thus be doubly determined, he is, however, much more reluctant to accept that a proper name can be doubly determined via pronominal suffixes. It seems that he is defying grammatical logic when he writes "further, the use of a name in the construct state is not the same as the use of a name with a pronominal suffix, even if the existence of the former shows that it is possible for a name to be doubly determinate; and we still have no other example of the latter. A difficulty may have been eased, but the suggested construction [such as the words 'his Asherah' in the KA inscriptions] remains unattested elsewhere in Hebrew."[34] This argument is clearly based on an argument from silence, since the fact that the construction in question is unattested elsewhere does not mean that it could not have existed—there is always a first time. Moreover, as will be discussed further on in this chapter there is in fact one instance in the Hebrew Bible itself where a pronominal suffix is attached to a proper name. However, in all fairness to Emerton it should also be pointed out that he himself very astutely noted that "not all idioms used in ancient Israel are attested in the Old Testament"[35]

[32]Joüon and Muraoka 2006: 452 n. 1.

[33]Emerton 1999: 325.

[34]Emerton 1999: 326.

[35]Emerton 1999: 332. He actually wrote this statement with reference to the fact that Brown, Driver, and Briggs (1906: 138) remark that the verb *brk* is followed by the preposition *lāmed* when the verb is in the passive, whereas at KA the verb is active. Be that as it may, Emerton's statement is valid per se and can be applied to different phenomena of Hebrew grammar and usage.

with the obvious implication that we could have at KA a phrase such as "by his Asherah" (Asherah here referring to the proper name of the Canaanite goddess). And even more pertinent (from the methodological point of view) to the discussion as to whether in Hebrew a personal name could or could not have a pronominal suffix attached to it, is what Emerton himself wrote, namely that "in view of what was said above about the syntax of 'Yahweh of Samaria' and 'Yahweh of Teman', we should perhaps hesitate to be too dogmatic in stating what was not possible in Hebrew, and we must be prepared to modify our opinions in the light of new evidence".[36]

In fact, in a recent study, Peter Stein has amply shown that in the light of Epigraphic South Arabian (henceforth ESA) parallels it is logical to claim that it is indeed possible in Hebrew to have a personal name with a pronominal suffix attached to it. Stein presented and discussed the relevant data that showed that the Old Arabian inscriptions contain a good deal of evidence that a divine name can be used as a *nomen regens* followed by a *nomen rectum* in the genitive, and that the latter could be in the form of either a place name, or another divine name, or a possessive pronoun attached to the divine name.[37] When applied to west Semitic, this could mean that the three cases just mentioned are exemplified respectively as follows: (1) "Yahweh of Samaria"/"Yahweh of Teman" (in the KA inscriptions); (2) *štr kmš* (in Moabite); and (3) "Yahweh and his Asherah" (in the KA inscriptions). Admittedly Hebrew and ESA are not the same language, and what obtains in one language does not necessarily have to be found in the other, but comparative Semitic philology does have a role to play, on condition that we exercise great caution when applying the grammatical rules and linguistic usage gleaned from one language to another and that above all the principles that we apply do function and clarify the actual usage of the language that we are trying to elucidate.

[36]Emerton 1982: 14.
[37]Stein 2019: 12.

The best parallel for phrases like "Yahweh of Samaria"/"Yahweh of Teman", where a divine name is followed directly by a place name without the use of a specifying pronoun in between, can be found in a phrase like *'aṯtar* [a goddess] *našq 'aṯtar* of Našq, the latter being the city of Našq(um) in Wadi al-Ǧawf.[38] An excellent parallel to *'štr kmš* on the Moabite Stone can be found in ESA in the phrase *'aṯtar sāmi'* ('Aṯtar of Sāmi') where the goddess 'Aṯtar is subordinate to the chief male god Sāmi'.[39] Finally, Stein provides multiple examples in ESA of a pronominal suffix attached to a divine name that would provide good parallels to phrases similar to "by Yahweh and by his Asherah" in the KA inscriptions. One very clear example in ESA is *šms-hw* ("his Šamsum [a goddess]").[40]

For Stein, the inscriptional evidence from KA shows us that "Der Gott Yahwe hat im Israel der vorexilischen Zeit verschiedene Kultplätze gehabt, darunter neben Jerusalem einen in Samaria und einen im "Südland" Tēman".[41] Moreover, the KA inscriptions are spared the zeal for monotheism that is shown later on in Israel since they show clearly that Asherah or her symbol was invoked. Indeed, the parallels from ESA teach us that we certainly cannot exclude that the phrase *wl'šrth* could be referring to the Canaanite goddess Asherah, and translated "and by his Asherah".

The problem is that, although the KA inscriptions could be adduced to support the foregoing translation, there is no way whereby we can be absolutely certain whether the person who originally jotted down the phrase *wl'šrth* had a cultic tree, namely the symbol of the goddess Asherah, or the goddess herself in mind. In the last analysis, whichever grammatical option—viewing the *–h*

---

[38]Stein 2019: 13. Although this is not the point at issue in this present discussion, still one should note that as far as the deity 'Aṯtar is concerned, we in fact have to distinguish between various deities: a chief male god of the Old South Arabian pantheon, and a female deity who could be venerated as an independent tribal goddess or as another goddess venerated as the partner of or as subordinate to other male gods (Stein 2019: 16–17 and references there).

[39]Stein 2019: 17.

[40]Stein 2019: 19.

[41]Stein 2019: 25–6.

as a pronominal suffix attached to a common noun (*asherah*, "cultic tree") or a proper noun (the name of the goddess Asherah)—it is the goddess herself that is ultimately being invoked. The reason is that, as Ryan Thomas says, "in the ANE, the deity and the cult icon were inextricably related: the icon was deity and treated as such".[42] Stein is of the opinion that the identification of the cultic symbol, namely *asherah* ("cultic tree") with the goddess Asherah herself led to the latter deity being later on degraded to a cultic symbol to the effect that *asherah* was tantamount to Asherah.[43] Later on I shall discuss in more detail the intrinsic link in the ancient Near East between a deity and the image whereby it was represented.

For now, it is interesting to first ask whether the etymology of the name of the goddess Asherah could be of any help in elucidating further the identification of the goddess Asherah with her cultic symbol, namely the cultic tree (*asherah*). Judith M. Hadley has shown clearly that "although various views have been presented, the meaning and derivation of the term [*šrh*] remain uncertain".[44] Notwithstanding this, it is important to note that the *Dictionary of Northwest Semitic Inscriptions* registers two lemmas for this word, namely *šrh1* and *šrh2*, with the former probably meaning "sanctuary" and the latter a "wooden sacred pole".[45] This last entry then, interestingly, leads to a further meaning, namely a "divine female consort". The dictionary simply shows this progressive meaning of *šrh2* thus, namely "divine female consort"[46] without any further comment. To my mind this means that a wooden pole (representing a tree) was taken as a symbol of a female goddess ultimately identified with the goddess herself who was the consort of a male deity. From the strictly linguistic point of view, this explanation still leaves a number of questions open, but it does help to underscore the fact that the sacred wooden pole that

[42]Thomas 2017: 172.
[43]Stein 2019: 26.
[44]Hadley 2000: 49.
[45]Hoftijzer and Jongeling 1995: 129.
[46]Hoftijzer and Jongeling 1995: 129.

was viewed as representing a goddess was identified with the latter. In other words, a common noun (meaning "wooden sacred pole") developed into another common noun (meaning "divine female consort"), with the latter still carrying a reminiscence of the original common noun, namely a "wooden sacred pole"[47] symbolizing a tree. There is in fact an iconographic representation that practically proves this point. I am referring here to a painting in the tomb of Sennedjem (19th Dynasty) at Deir el-Medina that illustrates Chapter 59 of the *Book of the Dead* and which depicts Sennedjem and his wife kneeling in front of the goddess Nut. This goddess stands in a sycamore tree "with her legs and the lower part of her body…hidden in the trunk of the tree". She offers the couple bread, fruit, and flowers whilst pouring water in their hands.[48] The tree is the goddess and the goddess is the tree, and, as far as the Israelites in neighbouring Canaan are concerned, given the evidence that we find in the Hebrew Bible it is logical to infer that for them the tree goddess in question would have been none other than the one known by the name of Asherah.[49] In

[47]Thomas upholds the opposite viewpoint, namely that originally, in fact "from the earliest of times", *asherah* "consistently" appears as a proper noun (for example, in Akkadian and Ugaritic) but "with anomalous usages showing up only later in Hebrew" (Thomas 2017: 193 and references there). However, it is important to note that it is Thomas himself who writes (ibid.: 196), "not only do many divine names appear to have originated as common nouns, but their meaning could change and evolve over time, depending on the historical and cultural circumstances".

[48]Buhl 1947: 93; Shedid and Shedid 1994: 41. For the painting, see the plate on p. 106 in Shedid and Shedid 1994. This representation helps us to counteract the viewpoint that in the KA inscriptions we necessarily have to choose between interpreting *asherah* as either a common noun (for example, "divine consort" or "wooden sacred pole"/"tree") or a proper name. As Thomas himself writes, "defying modern grammatical categories, deities could straddle the realms of proper and common nouns" (Thomas 2017: 181). As far as the Egyptian representation just mentioned goes, Buhl thinks that Nut's lower body and legs were hidden in the tree and that they were not part of the tree forming a composite deity (Buhl 1947: 94). Although it is true that the painting alongside the overall Egyptian evidence does not allow us to speak of a "composite deity", still it does not prevent us from concluding that the trunk of the tree can be interpreted as constituting Nut's lower body and legs. Be that as it may, in ancient Egypt Nut, Hathor, and Isis "played a major role in the tree cult" and it was the few male deities connected to sacred trees who "were never identified with the trees themselves" (Buhl 1947: 96); the female deities just mentioned were.

[49]Indeed, "the fact that 'Asherah' and 'the Asherah' occur in the same cultic contexts in the Old Testament (e.g. 2 Kgs 21.3; 23.4) indicates the close relationship between them. Accordingly, we may clearly speak of a close relationship not only between Yahweh and the Asherah cult object but between Yahweh and the goddess Asherah" (Day 2000: 60).

this sense the whole discussion as to whether *šrth* means "his *asherah*" or "his Asherah" in the KA inscriptions is either otiose, or has got to be regarded as a moot question, despite the fact that, as shown above, a proper name in Semitic could be doubly determined via a suffixed personal pronoun.

In Classical Hebrew, for example, a noun is definite when it functions as a divine name, or the name of a human person, or when it is a place name. Secondly, it can also be definite either by affixing the definite article to it or by adding a suffix to it (such as a suffixed personal pronoun). Finally, a noun can also be definite when it is in the construct state with a noun that is itself definite as a result of either of the two previous conditions.[50]

It should be noted that the examples adduced above, which show how even a proper name (whether divine or human) could have a personal pronoun suffix attached to it, were not from Classical Hebrew/biblical sources. Indeed, it is generally claimed that such a scenario does not occur in Hebrew, with the conclusion that therefore *šrth* in the KA inscriptions cannot mean "his Asherah". Thus, for example, J.C.L. Gibson states that "no proper names, place, divine or personal"[51] can take a pronominal suffix. Comparative Semitic philology, however, as already shown, does allow us to consider the possibility that such a construction could obtain also in Classical Hebrew. The KA inscriptions show that this is possible, but it would be ideal if we could pin down one clear example from Biblical Hebrew itself. Emerton had claimed that apart from the alleged instance in the KA inscriptions of a personal suffixed pronoun with a proper name ("his Asherah"), "we still have no other example"[52] of such a phenomenon in Classical Hebrew.

But is Emerton right? The first thing to note is that, although words that are definite in themselves do not take the article since this would be redundant, "there is one major class of exceptions", namely when the article

---

[50]Waltke and O'Connor 1990: 239.
[51]Gibson 1994: 34.
[52]Emerton 1999: 326.

endows a common noun with a unique status in such a way that the common noun in question together with the added definite article "becomes the equivalent of a *proper name*".[53] Such is the case with *nāhār*, "river", which refers to the Euphrates when the article is added to it. The same goes for *ba'al*, "lord", which then refers to the Canaanite male storm god Baal when the article is prefixed to it, namely when we find *haba'al*.[54] In this regard, it is interesting to note what Hebrew grammarians had already written back in the early twentieth century, namely that "all those proper names [such as that of the god Baal], of which the appellative sense is still sufficiently evident to the mind, or at least has been handed down from an earlier period of the language, frequently (often even as a rule) take the article…and may even be followed by a genitive".[55]

The foregoing observations include the name of the Canaanite deity Baal as one example of a proper name that could be rendered doubly definite by the addition of the article to it. John Day too has very clearly reminded us that "the fact that Ashera frequently has the definite article in Hebrew (*hā'ašērâ*) does not matter, since we likewise find Baal referred to regularly as 'the Baal' (*habba'al*) in the Old Testament, and similarly even 'the Tammuz' (*hattammûz*) for Tammuz (Ezek. 8.14)".[56] Since Baal can be doubly definite it should, in principle, be possible for this proper name to be doubly definite even simply by the addition of a suffixed personal pronoun. In the last analysis, as Godfrey R. Driver writes, "proper names may take pronominal suffixes, which imply the construct state", adding, however, "so far as I know, no instance of this construction occurs in the OT".[57] Yet, actually, it appears

---

[53]Waltke and O'Connor 1990: 249.

[54]Waltke and O'Connor 1990: 249.

[55]Kautzsch and Cowley 1910: 402.

[56]Day 2000: 43.

[57]Driver 1954: 125, who also gives examples from Arabic and Akkadian. Paolo Xella too has given ample examples, such as from Ugaritic, of cases where proper names can have a pronominal suffix attached to them; indeed, already at Ebla we have such evidence (Xella 1995: 607–8, 605–7).

that there is one case (of which I am aware) in the Hebrew Bible in support of such a scenario that would at the same time make it easier for us to accept the same type of construction as *šrth* ("his Asherah") in the KA inscriptions.

I am referring to Hos. 2:18, where we find the word *ba'alî* which per se means "my husband", paralleling *'îšî* in the second stich. However, given the overall context of this verse, *ba'alî* could simultaneously mean "my Baal". Indeed, Andrew A. Macintosh translates this verse thus: "And so on that day, oracle of Yahweh, you will call out 'My husband' and no longer will you call me 'My Baal'".[58] As such there is no distinction in usage between the word *ba'al* and *'îš*: they are synonyms for "husband".[59] However, in the context of the book of Hosea it is clear that in 2:18 there is very possibly a veiled reference to the Canaanite male deity of fertility (who was also the storm god), namely Baal. In Hos. 2:18 we are dealing with a pun; as Macintosh states: "If, then, Israel had deluded herself by calling Yahweh Baal, by treating him as if he were the Canaanite fertility god of that name, it is likely that the titles *Ishi* and *Baali* are used here to define Hosea's attempt to correct that delusion".[60] The context fully supports this interpretation. However, for it to hold we have to accept the fact that the proper name Baal has the pronominal suffix attached to it, with the result that *ba'alî* also means "my Baal". Such usage is in turn supported by the comparative Semitic evidence mentioned above. Indeed, as Driver states, it is very important "not to attempt to explain the phenomena of one Semitic language without reference to the sister languages".[61] Be that as it may, Hos. 2:18 cannot be fully appreciated until we grasp the fact that *ba'alî* simultaneously means "my husband" and "my Baal". In a textual note to *'îšî* and *ba'alî* in Hos. 2:18 Ehud Ben Zvi could not have put the situation any better than he

---

[58]Macintosh 1997: 77.

[59]Macintosh 1997: 78.

[60]Macintosh 1997: 79. In fact, Douglas Stuart is correct when he claims that the oracle in which the word *ba'alî* is found is based on the fact that *ba'al* means "Baal", the Canaanite deity, as well as "husband, lord, master" (Stuart 1987: 57).

[61]Driver 1954: 130.

actually did when he wrote: "both Ishi and Baali mean 'my husband', but the latter also means 'my Baal'".[62]

So, we now have evidence from Eblaite, Ugaritic, Arabic, Akkadian, and Biblical Hebrew itself in support of the real possibility that at KA also we encounter a proper name with an attached pronominal suffix, namely *šrth* meaning "his Asherah", with the latter word directly referring to the goddess herself. It should be noted that not all scholars agree on this. Ryan Thomas, for one, does not accept such a conclusion on two grounds: firstly, because in the last analysis he still holds to the virtual grammatical dogma that no proper name can have a pronominal suffix attached to it, and secondly because speaking of "Yahweh's Asherah" "would seem to make vacuous any notion of proper names".[63] Yet Yahweh's *asherah* is precisely *his asherah* and not *the* Asherah; Thomas takes the *asherah* of Yahweh to be a common noun (such as "consort") with reference to a deity, namely to the partner of Yahweh, but without the mention of her proper name.[64] However, it was already pointed out above that there is no distinction between the goddess Asherah and her symbol, namely the wooden cultic pole/tree that eventually came to be identified with the goddess that it represented and who, for lack of a better word, was termed "Asherah". By the same token, in reality there is no distinction between mentioning the goddess Asherah by name or referring to her by the word "consort" (namely Yahweh's consort).

In view of the foregoing conclusion, Emerton's dilemma in having to choose between the meaning of the word *asherah* in the KA inscriptions as the cultic pole as a symbol of the goddess, or the latter herself, turns out to be no dilemma at all.[65] However, if one were to insist on such a distinction with respect to the two possible meanings of *šrth*, namely "his *asherah*"

---

[62]Ben Zvi 2004: 1147.
[63]Thomas 2017: 191, 178.
[64]Thomas 2017: 194, 197.
[65]Emerton 1982: 19.

or "his Asherah", then one would have to logically conclude that from the linguistic point of view the whole question is moot, since we have no way of knowing what the author of these words really had in mind. We simply do not know whether he intended to employ the word *asherah* as a common noun (meaning a "wooden cultic pole or tree", or a "divine female consort") or as a proper noun, namely the goddess known by the name of Asherah.

In this respect it would be interesting to see if the Hebrew Bible could throw light on the foregoing issue in order for us to be able to conclude whether *asherah* in the KA inscriptions is referring directly to the goddess Asherah or to her symbol, or whether it simply refers to her by way of the common noun "consort". Deuteronomy 33:2 could be of great help in this regard, despite the fact that in it we encounter what in the context turns out to be the difficult word *ēšdāt*. This biblical verse can indeed be of help on condition that first the problems surrounding the word *ēšdāt* are cleared up.

The word *ēšdāt* has proved to be difficult even for the Masoretes themselves. Indeed they split the consonants *šdt* into two words, namely *ēš* and *dāt*, meaning "fiery law". Such reasoning is testified also by the Vulgate, which reads *ignea lex*.[66] However, this does not solve the problem when we consider that *dāt* is "a late Persian loan word in Hebrew, and unlikely in this context; and the fact that the consonants of the alleged two words are written together as a single word suggests that the Massoretic treatment of the word is not correct".[67]

Attempts made by contemporary commentators do not really solve this problem. Thus, for example, Richard Elliott Friedman reads the consonants *šdt* as *ʾašdōt* meaning "slopes" (as in Deut. 3:17 and 4:49).[68] Indeed, he tells us that in these two latter examples, the word *ʾašdōt* "refers to the slopes of

---

[66]Note that S.R. Driver too breaks up the consonants *šdt* into *ēš* and *dāt*, translating these two words followed by *lāmô* as "fire was a law for them" (Driver 1902: 393).
[67]Mayes 1979: 399.
[68]Friedman 2001: 673.

Pisgah, east of the Dead Sea. In this verse [Deut. 33:2], YHWH shines like the sun coming from the east over Seir and Paran, in which case the slopes of Pisgah would in fact be at his right".[69] Hence Friedman translates the last colon of Deut. 33:2 thus: "slopes at his right, for them". But what does this really mean? Duane L. Christensen, following David N. Freedman in reading *šdṯ* as *ʾašdōṯ*, meaning "mountain slopes", translates the last colon of Deut. 33:2 thus: "from the southland to the mountain slopes for them".[70] Once again this translation seems to jar. The translations of Friedman and Christensen seem to be stating that Yahweh shone forth for the holy ones, namely for the divine council. However, when one takes into account the overall context of Deut. 33:2-3, it becomes clear that this is not what v. 2 is really underscoring.

In fact, it was Henrik S. Nyberg who through a very detailed philological analysis that included the consideration of comparative Semitic evidence convincingly showed that once we also take into consideration Deut. 33:3, it becomes clear that the overall context of v. 2 is one of Yahweh's supremacy over all other deities.[71] He upholds that the obscure *ešdāṯ lāmô* in Deut. 33:2 should translate into "diejenigen, denen אשדת ist" whilst at the same time rejecting the proposal of the Masoretes to split *šdṯ* into two words, namely *ēš* and *dāṯ* meaning "fiery law", which, as already shown above, has also been rejected by a number of contemporary scholars. Taking into consideration the fact that the Septuagint translates *šdṯ* as "angels"[72] and that in pre-exilic Israel the written form of the letters *dāleṯ* and *rêš* were extremely similar, Nyberg

---

[69]Friedman 2001: 673.

[70]Christensen 2002: 836.

[71]Nyberg 1938: 337, 338, 344.

[72]With respect to this particular piece of evidence from the Septuagint, it is interesting to note that there are actually instances in this version where the word *aggeloi* translates *ēl* or *ʾlōhîm* (McCarthy 2002: 130 and reference there). Thus, it should come as no surprise that for the highly likely original *šrṯ* in Deut. 33:2 the Septuagint opted for a word that could indicate a deity. The Septuagint translators would no longer have known who Asherah was, but they did clearly understand that in the overall context of Deut. 33:2 the difficult word in question, namely the highly probable original reading *šrṯ*, must have stood for a deity of some sort.

proposes to read *šrṯ* instead of *šdṯ*, vocalizing the former as *ᵃšērāṯ*,[73] namely Asherah (the goddess) but with the old feminine ending *tāw*. Thus, the last two words of Deut. 33:2 would originally have read *ᵃšērāṯ lāmō*, namely "diejenigen, denen אשרת ist".[74] The reference is to the holy myriads, namely the divine council mentioned in the preceding colon. The ancient versions (including the Targum Onkelos) were not able to make sense of the Masoretic Text of Deut. 33:2,[75] whereas Nyberg achieves this by making a defensible adjustment of the consonantal text, *šdṯ*, by simply substituting the letter *d* with the virtually identical *r*.

Carmel McCarthy supports *šdṯ*, arguing that the single-word reading "retains the three-word pattern of the other four cola in the verse [v. 2 in Deut. 33], characteristic of early Hebrew poetry".[76] The solution proposed by Nyberg, which does not actually do any violence to the Masoretic Text but which simply reads a particular grapheme as it would originally have been intended to be read, shows us that, although in reality the *Ketiv* (that is, the written form found in the Masoretic Text) could have very well been corrupt already when the *Qere* (the proposed reading of the text, usually marked in the margins of Hebrew Bibles) was produced, it is "*more likely*" that the *Ketiv* "had existed in an earlier unacceptable form—that is, in a form perceived to be unacceptable according to certain norms of orthodoxy in vogue at a later stage in the text's transmission",[77] in other words, that the consonantal text of the word in question must have originally read *šrṯ*, with a clear reference to the goddess Asherah. Thus, McCarthy endorses Nyberg's proposal that in Deut. 33:2 there was originally a reference to this deity.

---

[73] Nyberg (1938: 335) states that the letters *dāleṯ* and *rêš* "waren gleich, und es hing vom Wissen des Lesers und seiner Auffassung des Zusammenhanges ab, welchen dieser beiden Buchstaben er in jeden einzelnen Falle wählen sollte". See also Blenkinsopp 2008: 138.

[74] Nyberg 1938: 334, 335.

[75] Nyberg 1938: 321.

[76] McCarthy 2002: 128.

[77] McCarthy 2002: 129 (italics added).

One could argue about how best to translate in an elegant manner the five cola that make up Deut. 33:2, but the essential point here is to realize that the last colon of this verse contains a reference to the goddess Asherah and that it depicts Yahweh as having this goddess on his right. McCarthy translates this last colon, namely *mîmînô ʾēšdāṯ* [but reading *šdṯ* as *šrṯ* with this latter word referring to the goddess Asherah] *lāmô* thus: "At his right hand Asherah for them [the holy myriads of the preceding colon]".[78] But what does this really mean?

McCarthy's proposed translation will make sense only if we keep in mind the fact that, although *lāmô* in Classical Hebrew generally means "to/for them", there are instances in the Hebrew Bible when it actually refers to a third person singular with the meaning "to/for him".[79] In such a case, we could translate the last colon of Deut. 33:2 thus: "At his right hand [is] Asherah for him [namely Yahweh]". But to say "At his right hand [is] Asherah for him" is the Hebrew way of saying "At his right hand [is] his Asherah".[80] And given the above-mentioned overall context of Deut. 33:2 it is clear that in this case the reading *šrṯ* refers to the goddess by that name (Asherah) and is not being used as a common noun.[81] McCarthy sums up the situation admirably when

---

[78]McCarthy 2002: 131.

[79]Kautzsch and Cowley 1910: 302 n. 3.

[80]The preposition *lāmeḏ* in the word *lāmô* in the last colon of Deut. 33:2 is not to be analysed as a "*dativus ethicus*" (Nyberg 1938: 330) but as indicating "only a relationship of belonging" (Merwe, Naudé, and Kroeze 2017: 348); "for him" here means "his". For a similar construction, see Song 2:16: *dôdî lî waʾănî lô*, which literally means "My beloved [is] to me, and I am to him", that is to say, somewhat more idiomatically "My beloved is mine, and I am his" (see Stern 2004: 1569). As far as the so-called *dativus ethicus* is concerned, it is preferable to avoid this term owing to the fact that the meaning is not really clear. For linguists, the *dativus ethicus* (ethic or ethical dative) is "used in referring to someone with an interest in or indirectly affected by an action, etc." and thus it resembles the dative of advantage or disadvantage (Matthews 1997: 118). For Hebrew grammarians the *dativus ethicus* is not identical to the dative of advantage or disadvantage, but it somehow constitutes "a special variety" thereof (Waltke and O'Connor 1990: 208). In practice, the *dativus ethicus* refers to the re-identification of an addressee "in terms of his/her current location (e.g. you, there where you are now) and directed to relocate, i.e. get *away* from where you are now"; such an idea of "actualization" could be metaphorical (Merwe, Naudé, and Kroeze 2017: 354).

[81]This is so despite the fact that the definite article is not used here with the common noun *asherah* to refer to the goddess, namely Asherah. Note 55 made reference to a citation that already showed that

she writes with reference to Deut. 33:2 that "one might suggest a theophany of YHWH, who is described in cola 1-3 as shining forth from three significant mountains, surrounded in colon 4 with 'some of the holy myriads', and in colon 5 with 'Asherah (or: Asherot) on his right'".[82]

The foregoing discussion shows that without doing any violence to the Masoretic Text of the last colon of Deut. 33:2 we can read in this colon the equivalent of the phrase "his Asherah" appearing in the KA inscriptions. In this latter instance, the evidence from the texts retrieved in the excavations at KA was ambiguous as to whether *šrt* in *šrth* was actually referring to a common noun, namely "consort" or "cultic wooden pole/tree", or to the goddess by the name of Asherah. The text from Deut. 33:2 shows that in ancient Israel before the emergence of a developed type of monotheism, and therefore in the pre-exilic period, there was the concept of "his Asherah", with the latter goddess belonging to Yahweh and therefore subservient and second in place to him. All of this tilts the balance in favour of interpreting *šrth* in the KA inscriptions as "his Asherah" rather than as "his *asherah*" whatever meaning one would like to give to this common noun be it that of "consort" or that of "cultic wooden pole/tree". This is a case where it is the Hebrew Bible that is helping us to understand more clearly the evidence retrieved in archaeological excavations, since in view of the foregoing discussion it seems that in the KA inscriptions *šrth* is best understood as "his Asherah".[83]

the addition of the article in such instances is *frequent* but it is not found in each case (see, for example, 2 Chron. 15:16 where the reference is to the goddess but where the definite article is not used).

[82] McCarthy 2002: 131.

[83] And yet, in view of what was discussed earlier on in this chapter, one should keep in mind the fact that in the ancient Near East there was no real divorce between a deity and its image. In this regard, Day is correct when he writes, "the fact that 'Asherah' and 'the Asherah' occur in the same cultic contexts in the Old Testament (e.g. 2 Kgs 21.3; 23.4) indicates the close relationship between them. Accordingly, we may clearly speak of a close relationship not only between Yahweh and the Asherah cult object but between Yahweh and the goddess Asherah" (Day 2000: 60). See also Doak 2015: 25; Emerton 1999: 333–4; and Greenspahn (2004: 483), who tells us that in various societies we find that the images of deities "were treated as if they were alive".

The evidence discussed in this chapter shows that we are really dealing with a two-way flow of traffic since we encounter two scenarios involving the interchange of the biblical with the relevant archaeological evidence. It is, in effect, a two-way exchange since at times (as shown above) it is archaeology that helps us to understand better the biblical text, whereas at other times it is the biblical text that helps us to gain a better and more precise understanding of the data retrieved in archaeological excavations. The corollary of all this is that it is incorrect to ask which of the two sets of data (biblical or archaeological) should be given precedence. In reality, precedence belongs to the research question. As Peters says, "the historian must give logical precedence to the question he or she is asking, as opposed to giving precedence to the document being studied".[84] When it comes to studying ancient societies, we have to use all the data available (analyzing them according to the rules of each pertinent discipline[85]) that act like different gateways to the past.

[84]Peters 2016: 31 and references there. Indeed, "the question sets the agenda, not the source, and the source is only 'relevant' when it provides answers to the question" (ibid.).

[85]It is clear that for such a scenario to be realized the scholar "must be well-trained [*sic*] in interpreting each of the given sources, something which is often missing in scholarship. There are too many cases of biblical scholars inappropriately using archaeological discoveries to fit their point, or archaeologists grossly misreading biblical texts to fit theirs, in both maximalist and minimalist camps" (Peters 2016: 31).

7

Conclusions

The preceding chapters will have shown that when it comes to relating the biblical with the archaeological evidence with respect to any particular issue that is pertinent to the field of both the Bible and the archaeology of the ancient Near East (particularly of the Levant), we can never be too cautious. I titled this study *Approaching Biblical Archaeology* precisely because I did not want it to turn out being just another of the many books (no matter how good) on the Bible and Archaeology, namely on "Biblical Archaeology", where multiple examples of archaeological finds are presented in such a way that they shed light on or confirm the Bible. My aim was different, since above all else I wanted to explain to the readers *how* archaeologists approach their data and, above all, *how* they reach their conclusions so that scholars (such as biblical specialists) can critically assess by themselves the reliability of the archaeological results that archaeologists pass on to them. The whole idea was to explain the essential approaches and thought processes of archaeologists in such a way that biblical scholars can understand what lies behind some piece of archaeological news relevant to the Bible (with examples mainly pertinent to the Hebrew Bible). In order to achieve this objective I selected the most essential facets of archaeology. I sought to offer a general presentation of the basic approaches involved, illustrating each one of them by at least one concrete example so that biblical scholars can then ask the right questions prior to endorsing or rejecting the information that archaeologists hand over to them.

In Chapter 1, after discussing what archaeology is ultimately all about, I showed how being *critically* aware of the results of the archaeology of the ancient Near East (in particular of those from the southern Levant) is not a luxury but a *must* (indeed, a *sine qua non*)—something that helps us to appreciate the biblical text itself much better. Thus, for example, it is on the basis of such critical evaluations of the data retrieved in archaeological research that we can reach conclusions with a high degree of probability that there were indeed such things as a pre-exilic Israel and a pre-exilic Hebrew language.

I then proceeded to show that one of the most important questions that we should all put to the archaeological information that we receive is: "What did the excavators actually find?" This led me to explain how we should distinguish as much as possible between the data retrieved by the archaeologists and the interpretation that they give to the data. I illustrated this aspect by the example (quite extreme, but absolutely true) of how further *examination and reflection* led to a radical reinterpretation of the underwater features found off the island of Zakynthos: the ruined city from the Hellenic period came to be seen for what it was, namely thoroughly natural geological concretions dating back to the Pliocene era!

In Chapter 3 I explained that all products that humans produce should be classified as artefacts, whether retrieved in archaeological excavations or not, and that it is useful to divide artefacts into two broad categories: inscribed and uninscribed. I argued that in order to gain good insight into past human societies all the evidence has to be taken into account, whether it is inscribed or not, and I also explained how the interpretive exchange between written and non-written evidence can take place in a methodologically sound manner. One of the examples discussed in this chapter was that of the Āl-Yaḫūdu archive and the archives of neighbouring towns in Mesopotamia that span the

Neo-Babylonian and Achaemenid periods, specifically from 572 BCE till 477 BCE. This archive throws important light on the Judaean community in exile, giving us a much clearer picture of how the Judaean exiles went about their lives in Babylon. As far as archaeological artefacts are concerned, I showed in Chapter 4 how their reliability depends on knowing their precise findspot location, information that can only be achieved on condition that the sites in question were excavated according to the principles of stratigraphic excavation. Indeed, the latter is crucial for a reliable chronology, even if often this is only a relative one. Relative chronologies based on stratigraphic excavation can in fact help us to argue properly when it comes to ceramic chronology. It is for this reason that I concentrated, by way of an example, on the much-disputed period of the United Monarchy in ancient Israel, showing how we should not marshal in the results of archaeology to uphold or to dismiss a United Monarchy before we ensure that the pertinent excavations were carried out properly. I also cautioned against drawing incorrect conclusions based on the absence of evidence. The upshot was that, when all the evidence is taken into account, it seems that in the tenth century BCE Jerusalem could very well have acted as the centre of a socio-political entity to be reckoned with, though not on as grand a scale as that pictured in the biblical texts.

In Chapter 5 I concentrated on the heart of the reasoning involved in the discipline of "Biblical Archaeology", namely on the special attention needed to avoid falling prey to circular arguments. "Biblical Archaeology" involves three aspects: the critical study of the biblical texts; the practice of archaeological excavation according to the rules of stratigraphic excavation; and, finally, the correlation of the results of critical biblical research with those of the relevant archaeological research, work done according to the highest standards of the field. It is during this third phase that special attention is needed if "Biblical Archaeology" is to be taken seriously. At times, as was shown, archaeologists have appealed to biblical scholars and vice versa in order to interpret certain artefacts without correct identification of these artefacts having been made by either side. The case of the *bāmāh*, a term appearing fairly frequently in the Hebrew Bible, was shown to be one notorious example of arguing in circles. However, I also provided an example from archaeoparasitology to show that "Biblical Archaeology" can be exercised without falling into the trap of circular argumentation. Indeed, the analysis of the faecal residues from toilets in Jerusalem dating to the sixth century BCE independently shows how dire the situation of the inhabitants of the city was—exactly as pictured in the biblical texts, notably Lamentations.

Finally, in Chapter 6 I argued that it is generally true that archaeology can throw useful light on the Bible, usually by way of clarifying the ancient cultural and historical background or at times even by helping us to better understand the semantics of the text. However, I showed that there is in fact a two-way flow of traffic going on since there are instances when it is the biblical text that helps us to understand the data retrieved in archaeological excavation. Thus I explained in detail how a critical appreciation of Deut. 33:2 helps us to understand much better the texts retrieved at the site of Kuntillet 'Ajrud that speak of "Yahweh and his Asherah". It was argued that it is highly likely that these texts were referring to the goddess herself and that the use of the suffixed personal pronoun with the personal name Asherah does not in fact (contrary to the common assumption) pose a grammatical obstruction to such an interpretation.

The foregoing specific conclusions reached in each of the relevant chapters have their own corollaries that can in turn function as final conclusions of a more general nature that have a relevance both for biblical and archaeological research, indeed for any type of research. The first thing to note is that the importance of making a distinction between the data retrieved during excavations and their interpretation (something discussed in Chapter 2) is valid also for biblical interpretation. Graeme Auld, for example, has discussed this matter with respect to the very early history of ancient Israel, specifically regarding the story of Saul. The "bare bones" of the story of Saul in 1 Samuel are: (1) that

Saul died with his two sons at Gilboa; (2) that at Hebron Israel asked David to become king; and (3) that the House of David had a tense relationship with Israel or with their kings.[1] Auld specifies the relationship between the "bare bones" and the "narrative development" of the story as being one where the former "are only *data*, and not necessarily *facta*".[2] This latter statement could smack of scepticism. However, if we remember that in the case of the story of Saul the "bare bones" are not simply "provided" but could also be "*deduced* from a now authoritative history",[3] then we soon realize that in reality facts are established and not given. As I pointed out elsewhere, "the human mind turns out as having a dynamic cognitional structure which passes through three stages: data, insight, and judgment"; it "attains fact by passing through the 'self-correcting process of learning' in such a way that the original assumptions themselves are duly scrutinized before facts are established".[4] In other words, we all give a provisional interpretation to the data before our innate "self-correcting process of learning" allows us to establish facts. This explains how the remains of the alleged Hellenic underwater city off the island of Zakynthos were eventually shown to be natural concretions resulting from geological processes. Indeed, as far as archaeology is concerned interpretation is often involved even in the very act of recording the data in the field, since, for example, archaeologists have to interpret the layers that they excavate before deciding where to draw the interface between any two layers.[5] And in the same manner, in the biblical example just mentioned, Auld has to decide what constitutes the "bare bones" of the extended story of Saul. As already

---

[1] Auld 2000: 364.

[2] Auld 2000: 364.

[3] Auld 2000: 364 (my italics).

[4] Frendo 2011: 57–8 and references there.

[5] This is so because "some interpretation is involved in the most descriptive statements" (Hodder 1999: 68). In fact, "it is more productive to acknowledge that the data are both constructed by us and that they objectively help to constitute our subjectivities" (ibid.: 62). Despite all appearances, this is not an endorsement of subjectivity as opposed to being objective, since, as discussed further on, the data are what they are; they cannot be objective, since objectivity pertains to our judgements and not to the data.

stated, this is not tantamount to relativism or scepticism, for the aforementioned "self-correcting process of learning" allows us to reach true conclusions on condition that we tread very carefully; indeed, "in the world mediated by meaning and motivated by value, objectivity is simply the consequence of authentic subjectivity, of genuine attention, genuine intelligence, genuine reasonableness, genuine responsibility. Mathematics, science, philosophy, ethics, theology differ in many manners; but they have the common feature that their objectivity is the fruit of attentiveness, intelligence, reasonableness, and responsibility."[6]

A second final conclusion of a general nature turns out in fact to be a corollary of the foregoing point but with special reference to archaeological reports. The issues discussed in this study push us to reflect further about the nature of archaeological reports. It is a commonplace that archaeological reports constitute one of the primary sources in archaeology, alongside the sites themselves and the artefacts retrieved during excavation. Since archaeology, of its very nature, generally destroys much of its own evidence, precise recording in the field is crucial since this is what will allow the data to be reflected in the primary reports, of which there are three types, namely current, preliminary, and final.[7] Current reports are generally "informal and non-technical" presentations of the data aimed at the general public; at times, these function as "brief technical or semi-technical reports" for specialists.[8] Both types of current reports are to be taken as highly provisional, since those who draw them up will have done so very soon after the discoveries in question were made, and thus without sufficient time for deeper thought and analysis. The preliminary reports proper are a notch above the current ones; they are "technical summaries of one or more seasons of excavation describing the

---

[6]Lonergan 1973: 265.
[7]Lance 1981: 53–6.
[8]Lance 1981: 53.

important results with some drawings, plans and photographs".[9] Preliminary reports are much more complete than current reports and they are usually addressed to scholars. Indeed, they are generally published in peer-reviewed academic journals. The snag with these reports, however, is that they often do not make any attempt to correlate the phases between the different excavated areas of a site and consequently it is difficult for the scholar to say something truly reliable about the occupational history of the site in question. For that they need to take into consideration the developments and changes that occur in the "current", "preliminary", and "final" report sequence.[10]

The so-called final reports generally bring together the data from all seasons of excavation, "publishing the finds in detail", correlating the strati-graphic evidence found in the different areas of a site, and building up "a coherent picture" of the occupational history of a site.[11] All this may sound very neat and proper, but in reality the issues discussed in this study (including some of the conclusions presented in this chapter) lead us to question what is really "final" about a final report. Since (as discussed in Chapter 2) there is a distinction between the data and their interpretation, and since "the self-correcting process of learning" mentioned above is what will allow us to eventually conclude what was actually found in any given excavation, it follows that ultimately it is only when we subject the final report itself to critical scrutiny and exercise our innate dynamic process of learning (which in the end allows us to establish facts) that we can really know what was actually excavated on a site. However, we have to keep in mind that it is not the data that are objective, since, as already explained, objectivity pertains to our judgement and not to the data. Indeed, as Hubert Darrell Lance wrote: "In short, interpretation of any particular archaeological datum is a continuing trialogue among the original publication, relevant new finds, and

---

[9]Lance 1981: 54.
[10]Lance 1981: 54.
[11]Lance 1981: 55.

critical commentators. One can never take the word of the excavator as final, no matter how imposing the 'final' report volume which contains it".[12]

This study has shown that one way to approach "Biblical Archaeology" is to come to this discipline with a well-stocked but open mind that respects our innate dynamic cognitional structure,[13] which allows us (via the above-mentioned "self-correcting process of learning") to know what archaeologists have actually found and how biblical scholars can integrate such critically established findings with their critical understanding of the biblical texts. In short, we shall be able to correlate the results of biblical research with our interpretation of the relevant archaeological discoveries of the ancient Near East (particularly those of the southern Levant) if we tread carefully, precisely, and with great attention to the data, going back to them in order to check whether our judgements are true or false. It is clear that our conclusions will stand in need of enhancement via further, ongoing research. In this manner it is possible to uphold a credible type of "Biblical Archaeology" without falling prey to an unscientific and naïve model of correlation between the Bible and archaeology, since "genuine objectivity is the fruit of authentic subjectivity",[14] with the latter acting also like a shield that can protect us from ideology. As Katharina Galor rightly points out, approaching data with preconceived notions and ideology "seeks credibility by posing as science, but its truth claims are based on strategies of interest rather than on objective analysis, a gap that can be intentional or not, conscious or unconscious".[15] As already discussed in Chapter 2, we need

---

[12]Lance 1981: 57.

[13]This is borne out by the fact that "no matter what its field of research happens to be, the human mind starts out with some inevitable assumption or theory and studies the available data with a view to understanding them. However, this is not sufficient for it to reach the truth; in order to do this it must check whether its own insight is correct, and if it turns out to be so, then truth is reached. A judgment must be made as to whether there is sufficient evidence for a statement to be maintained or not" (Frendo 2011: 57 and reference there in n. 23).

[14]Lonergan 1973: 292.

[15]Galor 2017: 5.

to distinguish between false conclusions and those that are true but incomplete. The latter can be enhanced only by further questioning and research. This, clearly, is an ongoing process.

My hope is that this monograph has helped readers to become more conscious of and seek to overcome the possible biases and prejudices that could cloud our judgements as we continue in our quest to correlate in a proper fashion the interpretation of the Bible with that of the pertinent archaeological data.

BIBLIOGRAPHY

Abraham, Kathleen. 2011. The Reconstruction of Jewish Communities in the Persian Empire: The Āl-Yahūdu Clay Tablets, in, Hagai Segev and Asaf Schor, eds., *Light and Shadows: The Catalog: The Story of Iran and the Jews*, Tel Aviv: Beit Hatfutsot, pp 261–4

Aḥituv, Shmuel, Esther Eshel, and Ze'ev, Meshel. 2012. The Inscriptions, in, Ze'ev, Meshel (with Liora Freud as editor, and John Tresman responsible for the English Style), *Kuntillet ʿAjrud (Ḥorvat Teman): An Iron Age II Religious Site on the Judah-Sinai Border*, Jerusalem: Israel Exploration Society, pp 73–142

Andrews, J.E., M.G. Stamatakis, A. Marca-Bell, C. Stewart, and I.L. Millar. 2016. Exhumed Hydrocarbon-seep Authigenic Carbonates from Zakynthos Island (Greece): Concretions Not Archaeological Remains, *Marine and Petroleum Geology*, 76, pp 16–25

Ap-Thomas, D.R. 1975. Review of P.H. Vaughan, The Meaning of 'Bāmâ' in the Old Testament: a Study of Etymological, Textual and Archaeological Evidence, Cambridge: Cambridge University Press, 1974, *Palestine Exploration Quarterly*, 107, pp 166–7

Auld, Graeme. 2000. The Deuteronomists between History and Theology, in, A. Lemaire and M. Saebø, eds., *Congress Volume, Oslo 1998*, Supplements to Vetus Testamentum, vol. 80, Leiden: Brill, pp 353–67

Barrick, Boyd W. 1980. What Do We Really Know about "high-places"?, *Svensk Exegetisk Årsbok*, 45, pp 50–7

Barrick, Boyd W. 1992. High Place, in, David Noel Freedman, ed., *The Anchor Bible Dictionary*, vol. 3, *H-J*, New York, NY: Doubleday, pp 196–200

Barton, John. 2000. Intertextuality and the "Final Form" of the Text, in, A. Lemaire and M. Saebø, eds., *Congress Volume, Oslo 1998*, Supplements to Vetus Testamentum, vol. 80, Leiden: Brill, pp 33–7

Becking, Bob. 2000. No More Grapes from the Vineyard? A Plea for a Historical Critical Approach in the Study of the Old Testament, in, A. Lemaire and M. Saebø, eds., *Congress Volume, Oslo 1998*, Supplements to Vetus Testamentum, vol. 80, Leiden: Brill, pp 123–41

Ben Zvi, Ehud. 2004. Hosea, in, Adele Berlin and Marc Zvi Brettler, eds., *The Jewish Study Bible*, Oxford: Oxford University Press, pp 1143–65

Berlin, Adele and Marc Zvi Brettler, eds. 2004. *The Jewish Study Bible*, Oxford: Oxford University Press

Black, Jeremy, Andrew George, and Nicholas Postgate. 2000. *A Concise Dictionary of Akkadian*, 2nd (corrected) Printing, Wiesbaden: Harrassowitz Verlag

Blenkinsopp, Joseph. 2008. The Midianite–Kenite Hypothesis Revisited and the Origins of Judah, *Journal for the Study of the Old Testament*, 33.2, pp 131–53

Brandfon, Fredric. 1987. The Limits of Evidence: Archaeology and Objectivity, *Maarav*, 4.1, pp 5–43

Brown, Francis, S.R. Driver, and Charles A. Briggs. 1906. *A Hebrew and English Lexicon of the Old Testament with an Appendix containing the Biblical Aramaic*, re-issue with corrections in 1951, Oxford: Clarendon Press

Buhl, Marie-Louise. 1947. The Goddesses of the Egyptian Tree Cult, *Journal of Near Eastern Studies*, 6.2, pp 80–97

Cahill, Jane, M., Karl Reinhard, David Tarler, and Peter Warnock. 1991. It had to happen, *Biblical Archaeology Review*, 17.3, pp 64–9

Christensen, Duane L. 2002. *Deuteronomy 21: 10–34: 12*, Nashville: Thomas Nelson Publishers

Cline, Eric H. 2009. *Biblical Archaeology: A Very Short Introduction*, Oxford/New York: Oxford University Press

Coogan, Michael D. 1987. Of Cults and Cultures: Reflections on the Interpretation of Archaeological Evidence, *Palestine Exploration Quarterly*, 119, pp 1–8

Coogan, Michael D., ed. 2018. *The New Oxford annotated Bible (New Revised Standard Version with the Apocrypha): An Ecumenical Study Bible*, fully revised and expanded 5th edn, Oxford/New York: Oxford University Press,

Coote, Robert B. 2007. High Place, in Katharine Doob Sakenfeld, ed., *The New Interpreter's Dictionary of the Bible*, vol. 2, *D-H*, Nashville: Abingdon Press, pp 824–5

Curtis, Edward Lewis and Albert Alonzo Madsen. 1910. *A critical and exegetical Commentary on the Book of Chronicles*, Edinburgh: T&T Clark

Dalley, Stephanie (editor, translator, and author of the Introduction and Notes). 2000. *Myths from Mesopotamia: Creation, the Flood, Gilgamesh and Others*, revised edn, Oxford: Oxford University Press

Darvill, Timothy. 2002. *The Concise Oxford Dictionary of Archaeology*, Oxford: Oxford University Press

Davies, Graham. 2002. Hebrew Inscriptions, in John Barton, ed., *The Biblical World*, vol. 1, London/New York: Routledge, pp 270–86

Day, John. 2000. *Yahweh and the Gods and Goddesses of Canaan*, Sheffield: Sheffield Academic Press

Day, John, ed. 2004. *In Search of Pre-Exilic Israel: Proceedings of the Oxford Old Testament Seminar*, London/New York: T&T Clark International,

Dever, William G. 2001. Excavating the Hebrew Bible or Burying its Origin? Review Article, *Bulletin of the American Schools of Oriental Research*, 322, pp 67–77

Dever, William G. 2003. Syro-Palestinian and Biblical Archaeology: Into the Next Millennium, in William G. Dever and Seymour Gitin, eds., *Symbiosis, Symbolism, and the Power of the Past: Canaan, Ancient Israel, and their Neighbors from the Late Bronze Age through Roman Palaestina: Proceedings of the Centennial Symposium W.F. Albright Institute of Archaeological Research and American Schools of Oriental Research Jerusalem, May 29–31 2000*, Winona Lake: Eisenbrauns, pp 513–27

Devries, Lamoine F. 2009. Politarchs, in, Katharine Doob Sakenfeld, ed., *The New Interpreter's Dictionary of the Bible*, vol. 4, *Me-R*, Ashville: Abingdon Press, p 559

Dijkstra, Meindert. 2001. I Have Blessed You by YHWH of Samaria and his Asherah: Texts with Religious Elements from the Soil Archive of Ancient Israel, in, Bob Becking, Meindert Dijkstra, Marjo C.A. Korpel, and Karel J.H. Vriezen, eds., *Only One God? Monotheism in Ancient Israel and the Veneration of the Goddess Asherah*, London/New York: Sheffield Academic Press, pp 14–44

Dillard, Raymond B. 1987. *2 Chronicles*, Nashville: Thomas Nelson Publishers

Doak, Brian R. 2015. *Phoenician Aniconism: In Its Mediterranean and Ancient Near Eastern Contexts*, Atlanta, Georgia: SBL Press

Driver, G.R. 1954. Reflections on Recent Articles, *Journal of Biblical Literature*, 73.3, pp 125–36

Driver, S.R. 1902. *A Critical and Exegetical Commentary on Deuteronomy*, 3rd edn, Edinburgh: T&T Clark

Dymond, D.P. 1974. *Archaeology and History: A Plea for Reconciliation*, London: Thames & Hudson

Eissfeldt, Otto. 1963. Neue Zeugnisse für die Aussprache des Tetragramms als Jahwe, in, Rudolf Sellheim and Fritz Maass, eds., *Kleine Schriften*, vol. 2, Tübingen: J.C.B. Mohr (Paul Siebeck), pp 81–96 (originally published in *Zeitschrift für alttestamentliche Wissenschaft*, 53 [1935], pp 59–76)

Emerton, John A. 1982. New Light on Israelite Religion: The Implications of the Inscriptions from Kuntillet 'Ajrud, *Zeitschrift für altestamentliche Wissenschaft*, 94, pp 2–20

Emerton, John A. 1997. The Biblical High Place in the Light of Recent Study, *Palestine Exploration Quarterly*, 129, pp 116–32

Emerton John A. 1999. "Yahweh and His Asherah": The Goddess or her Symbol?, *Vetus Testamentum*, 49, pp 315–37

Engel, Helmut. 1979. Die Siegesstele des Merneptah: Überblick über die verschiedenen Versuche historischer Auswertung des Schlussabschnitts, *Biblica*, 60, pp 373–99

Enns, Peter. 2012. Protestantism and Biblical Criticism: one Perspective on a difficult Dialogue, in, Marc Zvi Brettler, Peter Enns, and Daniel J. Harrington, *The Bible and the Believer: How to Read the Bible Critically and Religiously*, Oxford/New York: Oxford University Press, pp 126–61

Faust, Avraham and Yair Sapir. 2018. The "Governor's Residency" at Tel 'Eton, the United Monarchy, and the Impact of the Old-House Effect on Large-Scale Archaeological Reconstructions, *Radiocarbon*, 13th March, pp 1–20 (DOI:10.1017/RDC.2018.10)

Finkelstein, Israel. 2007. Digging for the Truth: Archaeology and the Bible, in, Brian B. Schmidt, ed., *The Quest for the Historical Israel: Debating Archaeology and the History of Early Israel: Invited Lectures Delivered at the Sixth Biennial Colloquium of the International Institute for Secular Humanistic Judaism, Detroit, October 2005, by Israel Finkelstein and Amihai Mazar*, Atlanta: Society of Biblical Literature, pp 9–20

Finkelstein, Israel and Neil Asher Silberman. 2006. *David and Solomon: In Search of the Bible's Sacred Kings and the Roots of the Western Tradition*, New York: Free Press

Flammer, Patrik [G.]. 2016. Email to the author, 13th December

Flammer, Patrik [G.]. 2017. Email to the author, 21st March

Flammer, Patrik G., Simon Dellicour, Stephen G. Preston, Dirk Rieger, Sylvia Warren, Cedric K.W. Tan, Rebecca Nicholson, Renáta Přichystalová, Niels Bleicher, Joachim Wahl, Nuno R. Faria, Oliver G. Pybus, Mark Pollard and Adrian L. Smith. 2018. Molecular Archaeoparasitology Identifies Cultural Changes in the Medieval Hanseatic Trading Centre of Lübeck, *Proceedings of the Royal Society B*, 285: 20180991. http://dx.doi.org/10.1098/rspb.2018.0991, pp 1–10

Forde-Johnston, J. 1974. *History from the Earth: An Introduction to Archaeology*, London: Phaidon

Fowler, Mervyn D. 1982. The Israelite *bāmâ*: A Question of Interpretation, *Zeitschrift für die Alttestamentliche Wissenschaft*, 94, pp 203–13

Fowler, Mervyn D. 1984. "BA" Guide to Artifacts: Excavated Incense Burners, *Biblical Archaeologist*, 47.3, pp 183–6

Frendo, Anthony, J. 2003. Bronze Age Urban Households of the Levant: How Do We Really Know about the Past?, *Antiquity*, 77, pp 604–8

Frendo, Anthony J. 2004. Back to Basics: A Holistic Approach to the Problem of the Emergence of Ancient Israel, in John Day, ed., *In Search of Pre-Exilic Israel: Proceedings of the Oxford Old Testament* Seminar, London/New York: T&T Clark International, pp 41–64

Frendo, Anthony J. 2011. *Pre-Exilic Israel, the Hebrew Bible, and Archaeology: Integrating Text and Artefact*, New York/London: T&T Clark International

Frendo, Anthony J. 2015. Theology from the Earth, in, Emmanuel Agius and Hector Scerri, eds., *The Quest for Authenticity and Human Dignity: A Festschrift in Honour of Professor George Grima on his 70th Birthday*, Malta: Faculty of Theology, University of Malta and the Foundation for Theological Studies, pp 217–28

Frendo, Anthony J. 2016. Israel in the Context of the Ancient Near East, in, John Barton, ed., *The Hebrew Bible: A Critical Companion*, Princeton/Oxford: Princeton University Press, pp 86–105

Friedman, Richard Elliott. 2001. *Commentary on the Torah: With an new English Translation and the Hebrew Text*, San Francisco: HarperSanFrancisco, a Division of HarperCollins Publishers (1st HarperCollins paperback edn. published in 2003)

Galor, Katharina. 2017. *Finding Jerusalem: Archaeology between Science and Ideology*, Oakland, California: University of California Press

Ganor, Sa'ar and Igor Kreimerman. 2018. Tel Lakhish (Tel Lachish): Preliminary Report, 16/04/2018, *Hadashot Arkheologiyot: Excavations and Surveys in Israel*, 130:http://www.hadashotesi.org.il/report_detail_eng.aspx?id=25415&mag_id=126 (last accessed on 10th July 2018)

Gardner, Andrew. 2001. The Times of Archaeology and Archaeologies of Time, *Papers from the Institute of Archaeology*, 12, pp 35–47

Gelston, Anthony. 2010. *Biblia Hebraica Quinta: The Twelve Minor Prophets*, Stuttgart: Deutsche Bibelgesellschaft

George, Andrew [R.] (trans., and author of the Introduction). 2003a. *The Epic of Gilgamesh: The Babylonian Epic Poem and Other Texts in Akkadian and Sumerian*, reprint with minor revisions, London: Penguin Books (originally published in 1999)

George, Andrew R. 2003b. *The Babylonian Gilgamesh Epic: Introduction, Critical Edition and Cuneiform Texts*, Oxford: Oxford University Press

George, Augustin (trans.). 1958. *La Sainte Bible: Michée, Sophonie, Nahum*, under the direction of the École Biblique de Jérusalem, Paris: Cerf

Gibson, J.C.L. 1971. *Textbook of Syrian Semitic Inscriptions*, vol. 1, *Hebrew and Moabite Inscriptions*, Oxford: Clarendon Press

Gibson, J.C.L. 1994. *Davidson's Introductory Hebrew Grammar: Syntax*, 4th edn, Edinburgh: T&T Clark

Gignac, Francis T. 1989. Phonological Phenomena in the Greek Papyri Significant for the Text and Language of the New Testament, in, P. Horgan and Paul J. Kobelski, eds., *To Touch the Text: Biblical and related Studies in Honor of Joseph A. Fitzmyer, S.J.*, New York: Crossroad, pp 33–46

Gitin, Seymour. 2002. The Four-Horned Altar and Sacred Space: An Archaeological Perspective, in, Barry M. Gittlen, ed., *Sacred Time, Sacred Place: Archaeology and the Religion of Israel*, Winona Lake: Eisenbrauns, pp 95–123

Grabbe, Lester L. 1997. Are Historians of Ancient Palestine Fellow Creatures—or Different Animals?, in, Lester L. Grabbe, ed., *Can a "History of Israel" be Written?*, Sheffield: Sheffield Academic, pp 19–36

Gray, Richard. 2016. The Wrong Kind of Throne: Toilet Discovered at 2,800-year-old Shrine Reveals Biblical Tale of Desecration of Religious Sites by King Hezekiah, *Mail Online*, 28th September (http://www.dailymail.co.uk/sciencetech/article-3811712/ The-wrong-kind-throne-Toilet-discovered–2-800-year-old-shrine-reveals-Biblical-tale-desecration-religious-sites-King-Hezekiah.html (last accessed on 10th July 2018)

Greenspahn, Frederick E. 2004. Syncretism and Idolatry in the Bible, *Vetus Testamentum*, 54, pp 480–94

Gross, Simcha. 2015. Review of Laurie E. Pearce and Cornelia Wunsch "Documents of Judean Exiles and West Semites in Babylonia in the Collection of David Sofer", Bethesda, Maryland: CDL Press, 2014, in, Book Notes, in, *Ancient Jew Review*, 18th February 2015 (http://www.ancientjewreview.com (last accessed on 26 May 2016)

Hadley, Judith M. 2000. *The Cult of Asherah in Ancient Israel and Judah*, Cambridge: Cambridge University Press

Hallo, William W. 1990. The Limits of Skepticism, *Journal of the American Oriental Society*, 110, pp 187–99

Halpern, Baruch. 1996. *The First Historians: The Hebrew Bible and History*, Pennsylvania: The Pennsylvania University Press (originally published by Harper and Row in 1988)

Harrington, Daniel J. 2012. Reading the Bible Critically and Religiously: Catholic Perspectives, in, Marc Zvi Brettler, Peter Enns, and Daniel J. Harrington, *The Bible and the Believer: How to Read the Bible Critically and Religiously*, Oxford/New York: Oxford University Press, pp 80–113

Harris, Edward. 1989. *Principles of Archaeological Stratigraphy*, 2nd edn, London: Academic Press Ltd

Healey, John F. 1990. *The Early Alphabet*, London: British Museum Press

Hendel, R.S. 1996. The Date of the Siloam Inscription: A Rejoinder to Rogerson and Davies, *Biblical Archaeologist*, 59.4, pp 233–7

Henson, Donald. 2012. *Doing Archaeology: A Subject Guide for Students*, London: Routledge

Hodder, Ian. 1999. *The Archaeological Process*. Oxford: Blackwell Publishers

Hoftijzer, J. and K. Jongeling (with appendices by R.C. Steiner, A. Mosak Moshavi, and B. Porten). 1995. *Dictionary of North-West Semitic Inscriptions*, 2 vols, Leiden/New York/ Köln: E. J. Brill

Horsley, G.H.R. 1992. The Inscriptions of Ephesos and the New Testament, *Novum Testamentum*, 34.2, pp 105–68

Hurvitz, Avi. 1997. The Historical Quest for "Ancient Israel" and the Linguistic Evidence of the Hebrew Bible: Some Methodological Observations, *Vetus Testamentum*, 47, pp 301–15

Isserlin, B.S.J. 1998. *The Israelites*, London: Thames & Hudson

Joosten, Jan. 2016. Diachronic Linguistics and the Date of the Pentateuch, in, Jan C. Gertz, Bernard M. Levinson, Dalet Rom-Shiloni, and Konrad Schmid, eds., *The Formation of the Pentateuch: Bridging the Academic Cultures of Europe, Israel, and North America*, Tübingen: Mohr Siebeck, pp 327–44

Joüon, Paul and T. Muraoka, 2006. *A Grammar of Biblical Hebrew*, translated by T. Muraoka, revised English edn, Rome: Pontificio Istituto Biblico Editrice (originally published in France in 1923)

Kalimi, Isaac. 2005. *The Reshaping of Ancient Israelite History in Chronicles*, Winona Lake: Eisenbrauns

Kautzch, E. and A.E. Cowley. 1910. *Gesenius' Hebrew Grammar*, 2nd English edn, Oxford: Clarendon

Kennedy, A.R.S. and D.N. Freedman. 1963. High Place, Sanctuary, in, Frederick C. Grant and H.H. Rowley, eds., *Dictionary of the Bible*, 2nd edn, Edinburgh: T&T Clark, pp 382–4

Kenyon, Kathleen M. 1961. *Beginning in Archaeology*, 2nd rev. edn, London/New York: Phoenix House/F.A. Praeger

Knoppers, Gary N. 1997. The Vanishing Solomon: The Disappearance of the United Monarchy from Recent Histories of Ancient Israel, *Journal of Biblical Literature*, 116, pp 19–44

Koehler, Ludwig and Walter Baumgartner, rev. by W. Baumgartner and Johann Jakob Stamm. 1994. *The Hebrew and Aramaic Lexicon of the Old Testament*, tr. and ed. M.E.J. Richardson, vol. 2, Leiden/New York/Köln: E.J. Brill

Kuhrt, Amélie. 2000. Israelite and Near Eastern Historiography, in, A. Lemaire and M. Saebø, eds., *Congress Volume, Oslo 1998*, Supplements to Vetus Testamentum, vol. 80, Leiden: Brill, pp 257–79

Lance, H. Darrell. 1981. *The Old Testament and the Archaeologist*, Philadelphia: Fortress Press

Lemaire, André. 1998. The Tel Dan Stela as a Piece of Royal Historiography, *Journal for the Study of the Old Testament*, 81, pp 3–14

Lemaire, André. 2016. The Kuntillet 'Ajrud Inscriptions forty Years after their Discovery, in, Israel Finkelstein, Christian Robin, and Thomas Römer, eds., *Alphabets, Texts and Artifacts in the Ancient Near East: Studies presented to Benjamin Sass*, Paris: Van Dieren éditeur, pp 196–208

Levine, Baruch A. 2002. Ritual as Symbol: Modes of Sacrifice in Israelite Religion, in, Barry M. Gittlen, ed., *Sacred Time, Sacred Place: Archaeology and the Religion of Israel*, Winona Lake: Eisenbrauns, pp 125–35

Lewis, Theodore J. 2002. How Far Can Texts Take Us? Evaluating Textual Sources for Reconstructing Ancient Israelite Beliefs about the Dead, in Barry M. Gittlen, ed., *Sacred Time, Sacred Place: Archaeology and the Religion of Israel*, Winona Lake: Eisenbrauns, pp 169–217

Lonergan, Bernard J.F. 1973. *Method in Theology*, 2nd edn, London: Darton, Longman & Todd

Macintosh, A.A. 1997. *A Critical and Exegetical Commentary on Hosea*, Edinburgh: T&T Clark

Matthews, Christopher R. 2018. The Acts of the Apostles, in Michael D. Coogan, ed., *The New Oxford Annotated Bible (New Revised Standard Version with the Apocrypha): An Ecumenical Study Bible*, fully revised and expanded 5th edn, Oxford/New York: Oxford University Press, 1955–2007

Matthews, P.H. 1997. *The Concise Oxford Dictionary of Linguistics*, Oxford/New York: Oxford University Press

Mayes, A.D.H., 1979. *Deuteronomy*, Grand Rapids: Eerdmans; London: Marshall, Morgan & Scott

Mazar, Amihai. 2003. Remarks on Biblical Traditions and Archaeological Evidence Concerning Early Israel, in, William G. Dever and Seymour Gitin, eds., *Symbiosis, Symbolism, and the Power of the Past: Canaan, Ancient Israel, and their Neighbors from the Late Bronze Age through Roman Palaestina: Proceedings of the Centennial Symposium W.F. Albright Institute of Archaeological Research and American Schools of Oriental Research Jerusalem, May 29–31 2000*, Winona Lake: Eisenbrauns, pp 85–98

Mazar, Amihai. 2007a. On Archaeology, Biblical History, and Biblical Archaeology, in, Brian B. Schmidt, ed., *The Quest for the Historical Israel: Debating Archaeology and the History of Early Israel: Invited Lectures Delivered at the Sixth Biennial Colloquium of the International Institute for Secular Humanistic Judaism, Detroit, October 2005, by Israel Finkelstein and Amihai Mazar*, Atlanta: Society of Biblical Literature, pp 21–33

Mazar, Amihai. 2007b. The Divided Monarchy: Comments on Some Archaeological Issues, in, Brian B. Schmidt, ed., *The Quest for the Historical Israel: Debating Archaeology and the History of Early Israel: Invited Lectures Delivered at the Sixth Biennial Colloquium of the International Institute for Secular Humanistic Judaism, Detroit, October 2005, by Israel Finkelstein and Amihai Mazar*, Atlanta: Society of Biblical Literature, pp 159–79

Mazar, Amihai, 2007c. The Search for David and Solomon: An Archaeological Perspective, in, Brian B. Schmidt, ed., *The Quest for the Historical Israel: Debating Archaeology and the History of Early Israel: Invited Lectures Delivered at the Sixth Biennial Colloquium of the International Institute for Secular Humanistic Judaism, Detroit, October 2005, by Israel Finkelstein and Amihai Mazar*, Atlanta: Society of Biblical Literature, pp 117–39

Mazar, Amihai. 2009. The Iron Age Dwellings at Tell Qasile, in J. David Schloen, ed., *Exploring the longue Durée: Essays in Honor of Lawrence E. Stager*, Winona Lake: Eisenbrauns, pp 219–335

Mazar, Amihai. 2014. Archaeology and the Bible: Reflections on Historical Memory in the Deuteronomistic History, in, Christl M. Maier, ed., *Congress Volume, Munich 2013*, Supplements to Vetus Testamentum, 163, Leiden/Boston: Brill, pp 347–69

McCarthy, Carmel. 2002. Moving in from the Margins: Issues of Text and Context, in A. Lemaire, ed., *Congress Volume, Basel 2001*, Supplements to Vetus Testamentum, 92, Leiden/Boston: Brill, pp 109–37

McGlade, James. 1999. The Times of History: Archaeology, Narrative, and Non-linear Causality, in, Tim Murray, ed., *Time and Archaeology*, London/New York: Routledge, pp 139–63

Merwe, Christo H.J. van der, Jacobus A. Naudé, and Jan H. Kroeze. 2017. *A Biblical Hebrew Reference Grammar*, 2nd edn, London: Bloomsbury T&T Clark

Michaels, George. 1996. Dating the Past, in, Brian M. Fagan, ed., *The Oxford Companion to Archaeology*, New York/Oxford: Oxford University Press, pp 168–9

Millard, Alan R. 1991a. Texts and Archaeology: Weighing the Evidence: The Case for King Solomon, *Palestine Exploration Quarterly*, 123, pp 19–27

Millard, Alan R. 1991b. Solomon: Text and Archaeology, *Palestine Exploration Quarterly*, 123, pp 117–18

Montgomery, James A. 1951. *A Critical and Exegetical Commentary on the Book of Kings*, Edinburgh: T&T Clark

Moorey, P. Roger S. 1991. *A Century of Biblical Archaeology*. Cambridge: The Lutterworth Press

Na'aman, Nadav. 2006. Review of Mario Liverani, "Israel's History and the History of Israel". *Review of Biblical Literature* 7, pp 1–11

Nakhai, Beth Alpert. 1994. What's a Bamah? How Sacred Space Functioned in Ancient Israel, *Biblical Archaeology Review*, 20.3, pp 18–29, 77–8

Naveh, J. 1960. A Hebrew Letter from the Seventh Century B.C., *Israel Exploration Journal*, 10, pp 129–39; Pls. 17, 18

Newman, John Henry. 1871 (with introductory essays by D.M. MacKinnon and J.D. Holmes in the 1970 reprint). *University Sermons: Fifteen Sermons Preached before the University of Oxford, 1826–43*, 3rd edn, London: SPCK

Nyberg, H.S. 1938. Deuteronomion 33, 2–3, *Zeitschrift der Deutschen Morgenländischen Gesellschaft*, 92.3, pp 320–44

Olmstead, A.T. 1943. History, Ancient World, and the Bible: Problems of Attitude and of Method, *Journal of Near Eastern Studies*, 2, pp 1–34

Orton, Clive and Michael Hughes. 2013. *Pottery in Archaeology*, 2nd edn. Cambridge: Cambridge University Press

Parr, Peter J. 1962. Le "Conway High Place" a Pétra: une nouvelle Interpretation, *Revue Biblique*, 59, pp 64–79; Pls. I-V

Patrik, Linda E. 1985. Is there an Archaeological Record?, *Advances in Archaeological Method and Theory*, 8, pp 27–62

Pearce, Laurie E. and Cornelia Wunsch. 2014. *Documents of Judean Exiles and West Semites in Babylonia in the Collection of David Sofer*, Bethesda, Maryland: CDL Press

Peters, Kurtis. 2016. *Hebrew Lexical Semantics and Daily Life in Ancient Israel: What's Cooking in Biblical Hebrew?*, Leiden/Boston: Brill

Pitard, Wayne T. 2002. Tombs and Offerings: Archaeological Data and Comparative Methodology in the Study of Death in Israel, in Barry M. Gittlen, ed., *Sacred Time, Sacred Place: Archaeology and the Religion of Israel*, Winona Lake: Eisenbrauns, pp 145–67

Porčić, Marko. 2011. An Exercise in Archaeological Demography: Estimating the Population Size of Late Neolithic Settlements in the Central Balkans, *Documenta Praehistorica*, 38, pp 323–32

Postgate, J. Nicholas. 1990. Archaeology and the Texts, *Zeitschrift für Assyriologie*, 80, pp 228–40

Reinhard, Karl J. and Adauto Araújo. 2008. Archaeoparasitology, *Anthropology Faculty Publications*. 22. http://digitalcommons.unl.edu/anthropologyfacpub/22 (last accessed on 12th July 2018; originally published in *Encyclopedia of Archaeology*, pp 494–501, ed. by Deborah M. Pearsall. ©2008, Elsevier, Academic Press, New York. Used by permission)

Renfrew, Colin and Paul Bahn. 2016. *Archaeology: Theories, Methods, and Practice*, 7th rev. and updated edn, London: Thames & Hudson

Renz, Johannes. 1995. *Die Althebräischen Inschriften*, vol. 1, *Text und Kommentar*, Darmstadt: Wissenschaftliche Buchhandlung

Richelle, Matthieu, with a Foreword by Alan R. Millard. 2018. *The Bible & Archaeology*, Peabody, Massachusetts: Hendrickson (originally published in French in 2012)

Ritter, R.M. 2002. *The Oxford Guide to Style*. Oxford: Oxford University Press

Rogerson, J. and P.R. Davies. 1996. Was the Siloam Tunnel Built by Hezekiah?, *Biblical Archaeologist*, 59.3, pp 138–49

Römer, Thomas. 2005. *The So-called Deuteronomistic History: A Sociological, Historical, and Literary Introduction*, London/New York: T&T Clark

Roskams, Steve. 2001. *Excavation*, Cambridge: Cambridge University Press

Sass, Benjamin. 2010. Four Notes on Taita King of Palistin: With an Excursus on King Solomon's Empire, *Tel Aviv*, 37, pp 169–74

Schmidt, Brian B. 2006. Neo-Assyrian and Syro-Palestinian Texts, I: Moabite Stone, in, Mark W. Chavalas, ed., *The Ancient Near East: Historical Sources in Translation*, Oxford: Blackwell Publishing, pp 311–16, 321

Schmidt, Brian B. 2007. A Summary Assessment for Part 4, in, Brian B. Schmidt, ed., *The Quest for the Historical Israel: Debating Archaeology and the History of Early Israel: Invited Lectures Delivered at the Sixth Biennial Colloquium of the International Institute for Secular Humanistic Judaism, Detroit, October 2005, by Israel Finkelstein and Amihai Mazar*, Atlanta: Society of Biblical Literature, pp 101–5

Sertillanges, A.G. 1987. *The Intellectual Life: Its Spirit, Conditions, Methods*, trans. Mary Ryan, with a new Foreword by James V. Schall, Washington, DC: The Catholic University of America Press (this new Foreword was published in the 1998 Reprint of the English edition of 1987; originally published in French)

Shafer-Elliott, Cynthia, ed. 2016. *The 5 Minute Archaeologist in the Southern Levant*, Sheffield/Bristol: Equinox

Sharon, Ilan. 2014. Levantine Chronology, in, Margreet L. Steiner and Ann E. Killebrew, eds., *The Oxford Handbook of the Archaeology of the Levant: c.8000–332 BCE*, Oxford: Oxford University Press, pp 44–65

Shedid, Abdel Ghaffar (with the assistance of Anneliese Shedid). 1994. *Das Grab des Sennedjem: ein Kunstler Grab der 19. Dynastie in Deir el-Medineh*, Mainz: Philip von Zabern

Schiffer, Michael B. 1987. *Formation Processes of the Archaeological Record*, Albuquerque: University of New Mexico Press

Spiegelberg, W. 1908. Zu der Erwähnung Israels in dem Merneptah-Hymnus, *Orientalistische Litteratur-Zeitung*, 11, pp 403–5

Stein, Peter. 2019. Gottesname und Genitivattribut? "Yahwe und seine Aschera" aus altsüdarabischer Perspektive, *Zeitschrift für altestamentliche Wissenschaft*, 131.1, pp 1–27

Stern, Elsie. 2004. The Song of Songs, in, Adele Berlin and Marc Zvi Brettler, eds., *The Jewish Study Bible*, Oxford: Oxford University Press, pp 1564–77

Stuart, Douglas. 1987. *Hosea–Jonah*, New York: Nelson Reference and Electronic Publishing (a Division of Thomas Nelson Publishers)

Thackery, H.St.J., Trans. 1926. Josephus' Against Apion, in, *The Life [and] Against Apion*, London/Cambridge, MA: Heinemann/Harvard University Press, pp xvi, xviii–xix, 161–411

Thomas, Ryan. 2017. The Meaning of *ashera* in Hebrew Inscriptions, *Semitica*, 59, pp 157–218

Torczyner, H. 1938. The Lachish Letters, in H. Torczyner, L. Harding, A. Lewis, and J.L. Starkey, *Lachish (Tell ed Duweir)*, vol. 1, *The Lachish Letters*, Oxford: Oxford University Press, pp 20–185

Ussishkin, David. 1980. Was the "Solomonic" City Gate at Megiddo Built by King Solomon?, *Bulletin of the American Schools of Oriental Research*, 239, pp 1–18

Vaughan, P.H. 1974. *The Meaning of 'Bāmâ' in the Old Testament: A Study of Etymological, Textual and Archaeological Evidence*, Cambridge: Cambridge University Press

Vaux, Roland de. 1970. On Right and Wrong Uses of Archaeology, in, James A. Sanders, ed., *Essays in Honor of Nelson Glueck: Near Eastern Archaeology in the Twentieth Century*, Garden City, NY: Doubleday, pp 64–80

Veen, Pieter G. van der and Wolfgang Zwickel. 2014. Die neue Israel-Inschrift und ihre historischen Implikationen, in, Stefan Jakob Wimmer and Georg Gafus, eds., *"Vom Leben umfangen": Ägypten, das Alte Testament und das Gespräch der Religionen: Gedenkschrift für Manfred Görg*, Münster: Ugarit-Verlag, pp 425–33

Wallace, Jennifer. 2004. *Digging the Dirt: The Archaeological Imagination*, London: Duckworth

Waltke, Bruce K. and M. O'Connor. 1990. *An Introduction to Biblical Hebrew Syntax*, Winona Lake, IN: Eisenbrauns

Watson, Wilfred G.E. 1986. *Classical Hebrew Poetry: A Guide to Its Techniques*, 2nd edn (reprinted with corrections in 1995), Sheffield: Sheffield Academic Press

Weber, Max. 1949. *The Methodology of the Social Sciences*, trans. and ed. by Edward A. Shils and Henry A. Finch with a Foreword by Edward A. Shils, New York: The Free Press

Wheeler, Mortimer. 1954. *Archaeology from the Earth*, Oxford: Clarendon

Whitelam, Keith W. 1996. *The Invention of Ancient Israel: The Silencing of Palestinian History*, London: Routledge

Whitney, J.T. 1979. 'Bamoth' in the Old Testament, *Tyndale Bulletin*, 30, pp 125–48

Williamson, Hugh G.M. 2015. History of Ancient Israel, in, *Oxford Research Encyclopedia, Religion*, Oxford: Oxford University Press (http://religion.oxfordre.com/view/10.1093/acrefore/9780199340378.001.0001/acrefore-9780199340378-e-20 (last accessed on 12th June 2017)

Wilson, John A. 1942. Archeology as a Tool in Humanistic and Social Studies, *Journal of Near Eastern Studies*, 1, pp 3–9

Wiseman, Donald J. 1993 (reprint 2008). *1 and 2 Kings: Introduction and Commentary*, Nottingham: Inter-Varsity Press

Wolff, Hans Walter. 1990. *Micah: A Commentary*, trans. Gary Stansell, Minneapolis: Augsburg (originally published in German in 1982)

Woodhead, Peter. 1985. *Keyguide to Information Sources in Archaeology*, London: Mansell

Wright, David K. 2017. Accuracy vs. Precision: Understanding Potential Errors from Radiocarbon Dating on African Landscapes, *African Archaeological* Review, 34, pp 303–19

Wright, G. Ernest. 1958. A Solomonic City Gate at Gezer, *Biblical Archaeologist*, 21, pp 103–4

Xella, Paolo. 1995. Le Dieu et "sa" déesse: l'utilisation des suffixes pronominaux avec des théonymes d'Ebla à Ugarit et à Kuntillet 'Ajrud, *Ugarit Forschungen*, 27, pp 599–610

Yadin, Yigael. 1980. [Was the "Solomonic" City Gate at Megiddo Built by King Solomon?]: A Rejoinder, *Bulletin of the American Schools of Oriental Research*, 239, pp 19–23

Younger, K. Lawson. 2000. Kurkh Monolith, in, William W. Hallo, ed., *The Context of Scripture*, vol. 2, *Monumental Inscriptions from the Biblical World*, Leiden/Boston/Köln: Brill, pp 261–4

Zammit, A. 2016. The Lachish Letters: A Reappraisal of the Ostraca Discovered in 1935 and 1938 at Tell ed-Duweir, 2 vols, unpublished D.Phil. diss., University of Oxford

Zevit, Ziony. 2001. *The Religions of Ancient Israel: A Synthesis of Parallactic Approaches*, London/New York: Continuum

Zevit, Ziony. 2002. Preamble to a Temple Tour, in, Barry M. Gittlen, ed., *Sacred Time, Sacred Place: Archaeology and the Religion of Israel*, Winona Lake: Eisenbrauns, pp 73–81

Zimhoni, Orna. 1985. The Iron Age Pottery of Tel 'Eton and its Relation to Lachish, Tell Beit Mirsim and Arad Assemblages, *Tel Aviv*, 12, pp 63–90

Zwickel, Wolfgang and Pieter van der Veen, 2017. The Earliest Reference to Israel and Its Possible Archaeological and Historical Background, *Vetus Testamentum*, 67, pp 129–40

INDEX OF REFERENCES

INDEX OF AUTHORS